PREDICTING
THE TURN

However belatedly, we've absorbed the new truth: in business, size no longer delivers security. Irrespective of sector, digital innovation can make the mightiest quake. Speed beats scale – but speed alone is not enough. **Major companies seeking a pilot to help guide them through the new turbulence will find this book of immeasurable value.**

—Sir Martin Sorrell, CEO, WPP

The future of innovation is all about connectivity. The largest brands connecting with startups, creating a flywheel of energy. I can't think of a single person more uniquely qualified to connect the dots and layout the playbook for making it happen. Others have written the book on theory, **Dave applies over a decade of real world experiences and stories that truly bring the concepts to life.**

—Tim Kopp, Partner, Hyde Park Venture Partners; former CMO, Exact Target

The impact of technology has dramatically changed the marketing world, but its impact is much further reaching. Technology has redefined the way brands build relationships with consumers and quickly eroded the significant competitive advantages that large blue chip companies once held. *Predicting The Turn* **gives you a look under the hood on this rapidly changing landscape between traditional brands and startups.** Interesting and insightful, this is a must read whether you work in company of 100,000 or 10.

—Adam Weber, Chief Marketing Officer, Dollar Shave Club

Dave Knox's energetic new book is a must-read for big brand leaders. He prepares big company leaders for the new competitive set that operates with radically different business models – and there is no one better to tell this story! Dave has operated successfully in both worlds.

—Jim Stengel, President/CEO, The Jim Stengel Company

Few people can meaningfully speak of both the entrepreneur's universe and the Fortune 50. Dave Knox's unique background in these two worlds gives him a perspective like no other. In *Predicting The Turn*, **Knox lays out brilliant-but-simple strategies for how large companies can meet their industries' inevitable disruption head on.** Through real-world examples of technology impacting even the most traditional organizations, he shows how the startups, software, and social changes these companies fear might just be their salvation.

—Pete Blackshaw, Global Head of Digital & Social Media, Nestlé

DAVE KNOX

PREDICTING THE TURN

THE HIGH STAKES GAME OF BUSINESS BETWEEN STARTUPS AND BLUE CHIPS

Paramount Market Publishing, Inc.

Paramount Market Publishing, Inc.
274 North Goodman Street, STE D-214
Rochester, NY 14607
www.paramountbooks.com
607-275-8100

Publisher: James Madden
Editorial Director: Doris Walsh

Cataloging in Publication Data available

ISBN-10: 01-941688-44-6 | ISBN-13: 978-1-941688-44-1 *paper*
eISBN-13: 978-1-941688-45-8

DEDICATED TO

My loving wife, Cindy Knox
I could not have made this crazy journey without you.
Always.

My children, Lincoln & Mylee
I cannot wait to see the mark that you make on the world.
Remember to dream big dreams.

My parents, Tom & Pattie Knox
Thank you for instilling my love of reading and writing at
an early age. Every day I've tried to *fill the unforgiving
minute with sixty seconds worth of distance run.*

CONTENTS

FOREWORD

Dave has been passionate about large companies embracing digital disruption for as long as I've known him. When we first met, Dave was a leading digital voice and advocate for P&G. A few years later I was fortunate to have Dave join Rockfish, where we have been the Digital Innovation Partner for some of the world's largest companies, like Walmart, Ford, and General Mills. Dave is one of those few thought leaders that have helped start companies, invest in companies, and lead companies, all while serving as a strategic advisor to some of the world's largest companies. No one is more uniquely qualified to write about the intersection of big business and startups, and the opportunities and risks for both.

Until recently most large companies still couldn't imagine how their businesses might be threatened by digital innovation. Since the Industrial Revolution, being big was an almost impossible competitive advantage to overcome. The balance sheets of large companies allowed them to own consumers' attention through limited and expensive media options, and anytime a potential competitor began to gain traction they could simply acquire them for a fraction of their market cap – which was likely the desired outcome for the startup. But those days are long gone. Media is distributed, cheap, and highly targeted. Venture capital provides startups with enormous resources and valuations. The world's best talent now prefers to work for startups, with their lucrative options, potential IPOs, and creative work environments.

Not since David defeated Goliath with a single stone have giants fallen so quickly. And the battle is just beginning. A combination of denial, arrogance, and short-term thinking has led to this present moment where almost every large company has shown up to battle holding the wrong weapon. They are still expecting hand-to-hand combat when a thousand stones are flying in their direction. And the one skill they need to succeed is the one thing that years of growth and bureaucracy have rendered almost impossible – speed.

Speed, not size, is the new competitive advantage. The time and resources necessary to start, grow, and disrupt an entire industry will continue to accelerate. Business today isn't a drag race where we all race in a straight line. It's not a NASCAR race where we all drive in the same circle. It's a Formula 1 race where every track is unique, has many turns in every direction, and requires the nimble balance of speed and performance, talent, and execution. Dave is your crew chief. This book is your manual.

Victory depends on it.

—Kenny Tomlin
Rockfish Founder & CEO

CHAPTER 1

A KODAK MOMENT

"Business is full of stories of companies that threw that last party just when their world was about to burn."

—Converse CEO Jim Calhoun[1]

THE EASTMAN KODAK COMPANY reached the peak of its stock market capitalization in 1997 at nearly $30 billion. A decade earlier, the company's global employment peaked at just north of 145,000 people. A true monopoly in its industry, Kodak captured 90 percent of the film and 85 percent of the camera sales markets in the U.S. during the 1990s. However by 2012, the company that made the "Kodak Moment" famous filed for bankruptcy and became a case study of being left behind in the digital revolution. The story might have had a different ending if Kodak's senior management had listened to a 25-year-old engineer named Steven Sasson.

Steven Sasson joined the Eastman Kodak Company in 1973 as an engineer. After he received the typical "new hire" assignment, Sasson was asked to explore practical uses for an invention called the charged-coupled device (C.C.D.), a new electronic sensor that gathered optical information. In 1975, Sasson employed the C.C.D. and developed the world's first digital camera, an eight-pound, toaster-sized contraption and would be awarded U.S. Patent 4,131,919.[2] When Sasson showed the technology to executives at Kodak, they said that Sasson could keep working on it; however, he could not show it to anyone. As Sasson later explained in a *New York Times* article, *"every digital camera that was sold took away from a film camera and we knew how much money we made on film."*[3] The brilliant engineers within Kodak invented the digital future for the photography industry. However, Kodak's management missed the technological opportunity of a lifetime because they were shortsighted, focused on their current business and not the future. It is a common situation in the executive ranks of many big companies. The average Chief Executive Officer is in the job for eight years at best. A Chief Marketing Officer is in the seat for around four years. Why kill the profits today for something that will likely be the next leader's problem? As Sasson put it: *"When you're talking to a bunch of corporate guys about 18 to 20 years in the future, when none of those guys will still be in the company, they don't get too excited about it."*

Fast-forward a few decades. Nearly every one of the seven billion mobile phones in the world has a digital camera; all of these cameras are based on Steven Sasson's original invention. The digital camera has greatly impacted our societies and cultures and the way we communicate. U.S. President Barack Obama awarded Sasson the National Medal of Technology and Innovation – the highest honor by the U.S. government to inventors – for *"the invention of the digital camera, which has revolutionized the way images are captured, stored and shared, thereby creating new opportunities for commerce, for education and for improved worldwide communication."* In 2000, when film still dominated photography and Kodak was at its pinnacle, the company announced that people around the world had taken 80 billion photos. Today in 2016, in the digital photography world that Sasson envisioned, people will take over one trillion photos. In the world of Instagram, Snapchat, and Facebook, online photo sharing has become the real business, completely replacing the photo printing business that Kodak dominated.

The film world Kodak was in vs. the digital world Sasson envisioned.

Kodak's story is not unique. History books are increasingly filled with stories where businesses missed a technological shift and, as a result, their fortunes changed dramatically. Kodak was just the first of many big companies that did not miss a shift because it was unaware of the change; Kodak missed the opportunity because it was unwilling to accept the inevitable fact that you cannot fight change. The

Businesses missed a technological shift and their fortunes changed dramatically.

result is that a "Kodak Moment" is no longer about capturing a moment of joy but instead a warning for all Blue Chip companies on the perils of missing an opportunity.

THE CHANGE IS DIGITAL BUSINESS MODELS, NOT DIGITAL MARKETING

"Until recently, technology was understood as a rising new vertical industry. But in the past two decades, technology has become a horizontal force cross all industries, driving both a renaissance and a reckoning in every sector of our economy." —John Battelle[4]

In 2008, I had the opportunity to be a founding member of Procter & Gamble's Digital Business Strategy team. Reporting to the Chief Marketing Officer, our corporate team of three people was initially positioned within the company's Global Marketing Capability organization. This P&G Capability organization develops and hones the best practices of brand building and has been the top marketer training ground for decades. The mandate of the new Digital Business Strategy team was initially capability development with the added challenge of building the digital marketing muscle of P&G. The ultimate goal: to make P&G marketers as great at digital media (banner ads, search, and social media) as they were at traditional media (TV, print, and shopper marketing). Eventually, the scope would expand into e-commerce; however, in those initial years the team focused on building world-class digital marketing expertise at P&G across our 5,000 global marketers and 300 brands. With P&G's focus on training, the first step was to build the best practices and standardized approach for how P&G marketers would approach digital marketing. The second step focused on building relationships with the leading digital companies with whom P&G marketers would execute these digital marketing best practices. These efforts delivered on their purpose. The P&G marketers we trained launched many celebrated digital-centric campaigns including Old Spice's "Your Man" campaign, which received over 100 million online views and became the #1 all-time most viewed brand channel on YouTube.

As I look in the rearview mirror at our efforts – and those of just about every other big CPG at the time – I cannot help but wonder if our target was not big enough. We focused only on digital marketing when perhaps we should have focused on digital business models. Do not get me wrong. It is imperative for every company to develop its digital marketing capability – as it is a cost of entry in today's business world. However, to use the words of John Battelle, we viewed digital as a "vertical industry" and we thought about digital marketing as a replacement for our existing tools for marketing to consumers. Even when we thought about e-commerce, it was just another type of retail channel like grocery or mass. The insight we may have missed was that digital was really a "horizontal force" that would rewrite the rules of not just marketing, but business as a whole. The disconnect is that entire companies and industries were intimately connected for decades as the way of doing business. For department stores like Macy's, it was the local daily newspaper and their weekly sales circulars. For Procter & Gamble, it was television advertising. These industries were so connected that they were woven into the basic fabric of how each did business. As a result, the decline of one has serious ramifications for the other. On the flip side, we are now seeing new companies and industries that are being created on the back of the internet. The rise of digital has proven to be about much more than just marketing and advertising; it is causing companies to question the very business in which they compete.

We focused only on digital marketing when perhaps we should have focused on digital business models.

Why do I say that? Consider some of the changes that we have seen over the past few years.

For starters, consider how business is rapidly changing for big companies. The Fortune 500 was first published in 1955 and since that time, 89 percent of the list has completely turned over. Meanwhile on the S&P 500 Index, the average tenure of a firm on the list in 1958 was 61 years; now, it is under 18 years. The turnover trend is even carrying over to individual brands at these companies; for example, in 2015 Catalina found that 90 of the top 100 CPG brands lost market share over the previous year.[5]

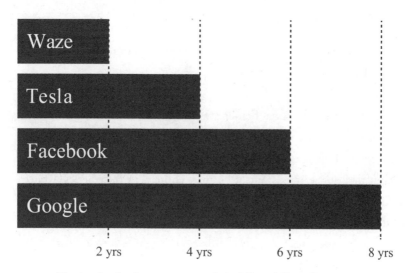

The time it takes for startups to reach the billion-dollar valuation mark is getting shorter and shorter.

On the flip side, new companies are growing at unprecedented speeds. It used to take 20 years for a traditional Fortune 500 company to reach a billion-dollar valuation. Even Amazon only had a valuation of $438 million when it IPO'd in 1997. Yet, if you look over the past few years, the billion-dollar valuation mark is being reached faster than ever. It took Google eight years; Facebook, six years; Tesla, four years; and Waze less than two years to reach that mark.

There is also the rise of what Andy Dunn, founder of Bonobos, called the Digitally Native Vertical Brand (DNVB). These are companies like Casper, the mattress company that delivers to your doorstep, which reached $100 million in sales in less than three years, and Dollar Shave Club that earned over $250 million in sales in that same time period before being bought by Unilever for $1 billion in July 2016. As Dunn describes it, these DNVBs share a few core characteristics:

- **Started on the web and are e-commerce driven**

- **Have a physical product**

- **Own their brand(s)**

- **If they have physical stores, they are experiential focused on engagement and service.**

In other words, traditional brands are facing new competitors that play from entirely different rulebooks and were born with digital DNA. These new competitors are not just trying to win market share; they are trying to put traditional brands out of business entirely. In their Series A pitch deck to investors, Dollar Shave Club captured this sentiment perfectly with a slide that stated its vision was *"Total domination of the global subscription razor marketing and become the largest online-only brand for Personal Care CPG's."*

The emergence of the Digitally Native Vertical Brand has been driven in part because the marketing funnel is transforming, not with the steps changing but instead happening much more quickly. Scale and distribution have historically been massive competitive advantages for Blue Chips, particularly in CPG where the importance of physical shelf space was at a premium and awareness tools like prime time TV were prohibitively expensive. When the internet, and mobile in particular, make it possible to purchase nearly any good from anywhere at anytime, it changes this dynamic. The change is even more profound as the middle of the funnel becomes digitally addressable as brands capture engagement and purchase intent in real-time. The result is that marketers have the ability to test against every step of the funnel while consumers have the ability to go through the entire purchase process in minutes, if not seconds. This leads to a landscape where emerging brands are combining the best of brand and direct marketing in ways never before seen. The venture capital firm Venrock wrote about this very difference of go-to market for "modern brands" in 2014:

> "But modern brands are born on the internet and sell directly to their customers, initially bypassing physical retailers, sometimes forever. They get to know their customers, they speak with them, they use social data to understand their influence and their habits. In short, they are hyper-informed as to who their customers are and what they want, and they have an easier time finding new ones. With so much of commerce moving online, customers prefer the convenience of direct-to-you product delivery and the low-friction of mobile commerce. Traditional CPG, like other industries who sell through complex multi-layer distribution, must allow for healthy distribution and retail markups and don't get to know their customers. They are slower to learn when preferences shift or to react to the moves of competitors. All of these differences add up to advantages for the modern brands built on the internet – price advantages, information advantages and most importantly, higher customer loyalty."

This quick rise of innovative new companies can also be seen in the emerging disconnect between the world's largest spenders on Research & Development (R&D) and those companies that are considered by their peers to be the most innovative.

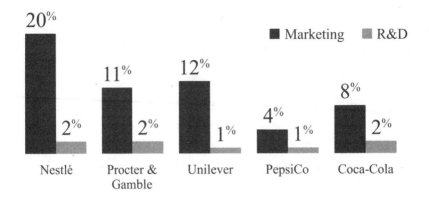

Marketing vs. R&D budgets of largest CPG companies.

In its Global Innovation 1000 studies, Strategy& identifies the top 20 publicly traded companies worldwide that spent the most on R&D and asked the Global Innovation 1000 survey respondents to name the companies they thought were the world's most innovative. Only five companies appeared in the top ten of both spending on R&D and most innovative – Google, Samsung, Amazon, Microsoft, and Toyota.[6] In the 1970s, the non-defense R&D budget in the U.S. was around $40 billion and the industrial world had famous R&D facilities like Bell Labs and Xerox's PARC. The venture capital industry started with approximately 20 firms managing around $2.5 billion. Today, non-defense R&D spending stands at $80 billion per year; but, the real change is in venture capital – over $165 billion is managed and nearly $60 billion in venture capital was invested in 2015 alone. Venture Capital has in many ways become the new R&D budget. The trend is not too surprising when you consider that R&D spending is fundamentally about brilliant people working on the cutting-edge of

Venture Capital has in many ways become the new R&D budget.

research. In the 1970s, the top graduates from MIT, Carnegie Mellon, and other top technical universities would all strive to get a job at Bell Labs or Xerox PARC. Today, those same graduates have grown up in a world where Startup founders are the new rock stars. *The Social Network* is their *Wall Street* and the best minds no longer have corporate R&D as their dream job. Their dream is to raise venture capital and follow the words of Sean Parker in *The Social Network: "a million dollars isn't cool, you know what's cool? . . . A billion dollars."*

The common thread in all of these industry transformations is the impact of digital. Not just digital marketing but technology as the fundamental driver of a shift in business and culture. In Amazon's 2015 Annual Report, Jeff Bezos captured this trend nicely when discussing the rapid rise of Amazon Web Services (AWS):

> *"Whether you are a startup founded yesterday or a business that has been around for 140 years, the cloud is providing all of us with unbelievable opportunities to reinvent our businesses, add new customer experiences, redeploy capital to fuel growth, and do all of this so much faster than before."*

These changes are part of what Robert Siegel and Aaron Levie brilliantly called the "Industrialist's Dilemma" during a class they taught at Stanford Graduate School in Winter 2016. The move from the industrial world to a digital one is "far more of a nonlinear shift" than big companies are accustomed to dealing with. As Siegel and Levie called out:

> *"It's one thing for a car company to react to a more reliable or more affordable car maker, as U.S. automakers dealt with in the 1970s. It's another to respond to the very threat of car ownership going away forever, or the challenge that making self-driving cars requires a fundamentally different skill-set from what you've invested in over a century.*

. . . These new digital experiences are inspiring customers to put major pressure on established analog peers. Most traditional players are not prepared to answer these calls. Slowed by heavy regulation, years of codified processes and aging technology, incumbents are burdened to the point where it is nearly impossible to move quickly enough against an unencumbered challenger. This is the Industrialist's Dilemma: the systems, management and assets that led to success in the industrial era are holding incumbents back today, in some cases fatally.[7]

Digital has become a medium that entrepreneurs and startups are using to attack incumbents in ways they never envisioned.

STARTUPS ARE THE DOMINOS

"Not every industry was made to last forever."

—Intel's Les Valdez to Interscope's Jimmy Iovine in 2002 regarding music industry/Napster[8]

In 1983, Lorne Whitehead, a physicist from the University of British Columbia was looking for a "simple and dramatic demonstration of exponential growth, such as in a nuclear chain reaction." In an article published in the American Journal of Physics, Whitehead proved that he could knock down the Empire State Building with 29 dominos. He demonstrated that a domino can knock over another domino one-and-a-half times its size. Through a chain reaction, it would take just 29 progressively larger dominos to knock down the 1,250-foot-tall Empire State Building. As Kodak learned, technology can be that first domino for a big company. While the threat might appear small at first and the change far off, it is actually a danger that can take down even the biggest of companies.

The changes happening across all industries are dominos that are starting to fall. Behind many of those dominos are startups and entrepreneurs, who truly believe that they can take down Empire State-sized companies and redefine entire industries. As Kodak showed,

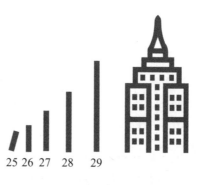

25 26 27 28   29

it's easy for disruption to be someone else's job – until you wake up and the disruption is staring you in the face. Big companies self-admittedly move slowly; yet, the change to their business is happening every single day. The first changes that happen take place in small increments that are often hardly noticeable. They also go unnoticed because sometimes the change happens when the base business has never been better. For example, the automotive industry had record sales in Q4 2015; yet the lowest number of 16-year-olds, ever, got their drivers' licenses that year.

Low teen driver rates could be the first domino in the automotive industry.

The issue is that the domino theory proved change is not linear, it is exponential. Exponential growth is at the heart of the technology industry. Google famously aims for "10x, not 10 percent" in not only their core product offerings but also their "moonshot" projects like the self-driving car. Venture Capitalists, particularly those investing in

Software as a Service (SaaS) companies, challenge their companies to aim for "triple, triple, double, double, double," (T2D3 for short), referring to a company's annualized growth to exponentially go from $2MM to $100MM+ in revenue over a five year period. For innovative technology companies, consistent and linear growth is actually not growth at all. Growth is exponential.

"Tech companies will eventually displace the majority of the Fortune 500. Competing without software is like competing without electricity."
—Navel Ravikant Co-Founder of AngelList

As such, big companies need to forget what they knew about competition because the new competitors will be following the exponential mantra of the technology industry. Business used to operate in a world of leader vs. challenger: Coke vs. Pepsi, Ford vs. General Motors, UPS vs. FedEx. It was all a battle for market share and growth or decline was often linear. In this new exponential world, disruptive innovators are no longer content to define themselves by a single market; they think bigger. They are not content with having a slice of a market. They want the whole market and often something bigger. Steve Blank contrasted this very difference between Startups and Blue Chips when he wrote:

> *"Startups are unencumbered by the status quo. They re-envision how an industry can operate and grow, and they focus on better value propositions. On the low-end, they undercut cost structures, resulting in customer migration. At the high-end they create products and services that never existed before. As we've seen, corporations are very good at maintaining, defending and refining existing business models, and they're pretty good at extending existing models by identifying adjacencies. But corporations are weak, and have become weaker, in identifying new disruption opportunities."*

The result is that corporations are faced with a new class of rivals. These rivals are now everywhere and not the ones you have known in the past.

PREDICTING THE TURN IN HIGH STAKES BUSINESS

"Every moment in business happens only once. The next Bill Gates will not build an operating system. The next Larry Page or Sergey Brin won't make a search engine. And the next Mark Zuckerberg won't create a social network. If you are copying these guys, you aren't learning from them." —Peter Thiel in *Zero to One*

The term "high stakes" is most often associated with the card game of poker. In a parallel to poker, Blue Chips are now in a game of high stakes business with disruptive startups. In high stakes business, the rules and players of the game have changed. The game has become high stakes because these new players are not looking for just market share, they are looking to make your business obsolete. They want to take down the entire table.

For marketers and big company executives, the answer lies in how to play this new high stakes game of business. The goal of this book is to provide you a plan to do just that, built upon my unique worldview and experiences working across big brands, startups and venture capital. During the first seven years of my career, I experienced the early innings of the change digital was bringing to the Fortune 500 as a Brand Manager at Procter & Gamble. In the last seven years as the Chief Marketing Officer of Rockfish, I have spent my days working with Blue Chip companies such as Ford Motor Company, Walmart, and Mars to confront this new disruptive business landscape. My nights and weekends over this same time period have been spent in the entrepreneurial world as co-founder of The Brandery, one of the top ten startup accelerators in the U.S. Finally, the remaining time is spent working within the world of Venture Capital, both as an advisor to several leading venture funds but also as a managing partner of a micro VC called Vine St. Ventures.

These three "jobs" allow me to see different sides of the same chip. During the days, I see the Industrialist Dilemma playing out first-hand as some of the world's largest brands and companies face a new reality and constantly changing landscape. At night, I see the entrepreneurial journey playing out as Startups look to beat seemingly impossible odds as they build a new business. The result is a seemingly unique – though at times conflicted – view into how big companies think about innovation and how startups and investors approach the very same topic.

The chapters that follow will provide the roadmap to win in this new game of business. At the end, you will be able to turn the threats into your company's advantage. It will start by looking at the concept of "seeing the future" and how participating in the startup ecosystem can help a company see the future of its industry before it happens. It will then cover four specific strategies that a company might implement, including:

ACQUIRE Innovation-driven acquisition where a smaller company is purchased to move forward strategic goals of the company.

INVEST Making a financial investment into a startup to further both strategic and financial goals.

PARTNER   Leveraging strategic business development and joint business planning to collaborate with small and large companies.

BUILD   Disrupt the disruptor by building a competitive solution inspired by current innovators.

Those are merely the tactics that will be discussed. These pages are meant to spur your own thinking on where the future is headed and the opportunities created along that journey of discovery. More importantly, it is about increasing your odds of winning in the game of high stakes business by predicting the turn.

In a parallel to another type of high stakes game, the "Turn" is the name for the fourth card dealt face-up on the board, in community card poker games like Texas Hold'em and Omaha. It can be thought of the midpoint of any given hand. In poker strategy, the Turn is often ignored with more attention paid to how you should behave at the Flop (when cards one through three are shown) or the River (when the fifth / last card is shown). If you are still in the game at the Turn, it means you felt like you had a strong hand after the first three cards were shown at the Flop. As a result, the Turn is arguably when the hardest decision comes to either continue to fight for the hand or to let it go. The Turn is also when the game can change and the person who felt they were winning the hand might just now find themselves playing from behind.

Predicting The Turn is about this difficult decision when the stakes are raised and you are in the middle of a high stakes game of business.

Whether they know it or not, every Blue Chip company is in a high stakes games of business against new innovative startups. While it is becoming increasingly challenging for mature companies to compete with these younger competitors regarding innovation, that does not mean it is time to fold. By taking the right steps, big companies can improve their odds against startups and predict the turn. This book is about putting your company in a position where you have the best odds to win in high stakes business.

"The sooner you stop fighting the present, the sooner you can get to work on figuring out the future."

—David Heinemeier Hansson, Creator of Ruby on Rails and Founder/CTO of Basecamp[9]

EVERYTHING BUT THE HOUSE

Quietly born in the Midwest, Everything But The House has quickly emerged as the world's largest estate sale marketplace. EBTH is simultaneously challenging traditional businesses like Christie's and Sotheby's that are over 200 years old, while also disrupting newer digital innovators like eBay. Eight years in business and EBTH continues to grow top-line revenues by more than 2x year after year – and is positioned to quickly become the predominant marketplace for buying and selling anything secondhand. Founder / Partner Brian Graves:

When Everything But The House (EBTH.com) launched our first online estate sale in early 2008, it wasn't just a matter of being "online" that made it successful. By then, eBay had already been facilitating the sale of second-hand goods for well over a decade.

By 2004, a significant number of new businesses were cropping up in strip malls around the country, offering services to represent sellers by navigating existing online platforms to sell items that owners no longer had a need for. But when it came to facilitating the sale of an entire home's contents, neither of these offerings tackled the greater need. For an individual to use a marketplace similar to eBay, they had to place their life on hold, and become an expert in the items and the platform, writing descriptions, taking photographs, determining how much to ask, and packaging shipments. And, if you wanted to hire a representative to do this for you, most businesses offering online consignment were not positioned to handle an entire home's contents, especially on short notice. In short, eBay became more of a place to go to look for something you needed, and less of a place to discover something you didn't know existed.

So, where did this leave the owner of an entire home's contents that needed to be sold? Well, at the time, it left them in the same place they had been for decades, if not centuries. Families were left with the option of trying to manage selling items on their own or working with a combination of consignment shops or specialty auction houses that might be willing to represent a portion of the items, albeit only the most interesting and valuable ones. Of course, there were options available to hire someone to represent the entire collection such as an estate buyout specialist, an on-site auctioneer, or a tag sale company. However, all of these options left something to be desired. Typically, the better items sold to a regional buyer that either got one heck of a deal or just turned around and sold it themselves, whether through a specialty auction house or online, for a profit. And marginally valued merchandise either wasn't sold or was sold in such large volumes which resulted in pennies on the dollar at best or an expense to dispose of at worst.

Enter Everything But The House. Even by taking on the name, EBTH staked our claim as to who we intended to be in this industry, even though that represented a seemingly impossible challenge due to the investment of human capital required, in addition to the need to create processes and systems that didn't exist. Most importantly, there was an insurmountable need in the industry that wasn't being addressed. We were facing one of the largest dispersals of second-hand merchandise, in our history, as the Baby Boomer generation began to downsize. And for the first time in decades, the supply significantly outweighed the demand, making pricing for second-hand objects a dynamic exercise. This was both due to the internet providing more availability to huge volumes of second-hand merchandise, and a new generation of consumers that placed less focus on collecting objects, as opposed to experiences. Comprehensive unmatched service + basic supply and demand enabled via human capital + technology.

Of course, like many great success stories the concept seems amazingly simple. But that was the idea, to take on the challenge of selling everything you might find in a home, over an exceptionally short period of time, while providing both the simplest and most lucrative outcome. All while creating a culture of raving fans. Doing that basically requires aggregating the best possible traits from all of the existing options, both traditional and progressive, in addition to introducing new ones otherwise thought to be unattainable or unsustainable. With this in mind, it's first and foremost about doing what is best for the client, and not what's best, or more appropriately, simple, for EBTH. As with any marketplace that represents both the seller and the buyer, it's about making it transparent, accessible, and enjoyable.

The primary challenge of our leadership is to in some cases identify, but more often, invent, systems and processes that allow for our service to be a sustainable offering, while staying true to our legacy of changing consumer's expectations. It's also necessary to understand that all of these represented challenges will result in an inability to be perfect. Disrupting an industry isn't about being perfect. If disruptors waited for everything to be perfect, they'd never be able to redefine an industry. What makes EBTH.com a successful disruptor is a willingness to forge ahead while looking at things based on how they should be as opposed to how they are, with a humble intent to offer a heartfelt experience that is better not only than any combination of available alternatives, but also better than our current self.

Disrupting an industry isn't about being perfect.

CHAPTER 2

CANARY IN THE COAL MINE

"Ultimately this allows venture capitalists to develop a sense of how and when the future will happen, and to share that foresight with key stakeholders throughout the corporation. The ability to see the future of your industry before it happens."

—Scott Lenet, co-founder of Touchdown Ventures[1]

BEFORE A COMPANY can make their first move in high stakes business, they need to understand not only the rules of the game but also the very nature of the game they are playing. Many industries, particularly those of the largest Blue Chips, have been relatively stable when it comes to the fundamental markets in which they compete. Car ownership did not really change from 1950 to 2000. Neither did the act of grocery shopping or fast food. In fact, this stability is what allowed many of today's Blue Chips to become the dominant global leaders they are because they could focus on expansion rather defending their core business. This stability has disappeared in the last few years. The result is that many Blue Chips are now in a game of high stakes business that they were not anticipating. The leaders of yesterday have to learn the rules of an entirely new game of business in order to maintain their position as the leaders of tomorrow.

The issue for big companies is there is no rule book for this new game. High stakes business is not necessarily confined by rules, the game board is constantly changing, and the future rarely looks like the past. This change is actually what creates the opportunity, but it requires a new approach. The first step is to build market intelligence. At a fundamental level, market intelligence is developing a sense of how and when the future will happen in a given industry. It is about understanding that in high stakes business, your industry and competitive set is likely much broader than the one you know today.

Consider the changes in Consumer Packaged Goods (CPG) thanks to Subscription Commerce. The business model of signing up for a monthly program where a product is delivered to your house is not a new concept in retail. For years, the wine industry relied on "wine clubs," which account for a significant percentage of the industry's revenue. In the mid-1990s, the music club Columbia House accounted for 15 percent of all CD sales, peaking at $1.4 billion in revenue.

Columbia House is an early example of Subscription Commerce.

Around 2011, this old business model was given the new name of Subscription Commerce. In Subscription Commerce, a box of products or samples is sent directly to a customer on a recurring basis, often monthly. The rise of subscription commerce started in women's beauty products (Birchbox is often credited with being the first break-out success) but has since diversified into over 30 categories including arts and crafts, pets, fitness and many more. In 2014, just three years after the trend started, subscription box services earned over $5 billion in revenue and grew over 200 percent in that year alone. Fast forward to today and several of those subscription box startups are now businesses that are generating over $100 million in revenue. In the $64-billion-dollar snacking industry, NatureBox had 2,000 percent growth in its first few years before crossing the $100 million revenue mark in 2015. In the beauty space, Ipsy has over one million members and north of $150 million in revenue. In the pet care space, Bark & Co. went from 49 subscribers in December 2011, to 15,000 in 2012, and to 100,000 in December 2013, in its march to $100 million in revenue.

Bark & Co saw exponential subscriber growth over their first three years.

Initially, many of the subscription commerce companies were new-age "retailers" where their boxes contained samples of other brands. The beauty box company Birchbox was a competitor to a retailer like Sephora but a partner to a manufacturer like L'Oréal. As they grew, the more progressive startups realized they had an opportunity to combine the margins of the retailer and the manufacturer by developing their own products and evolving into significant brands in their own right. Unlike other CPG companies however, they would own the relationship with their consumers directly because of their subscription roots. As a result, these subscription commerce brands have become noteworthy competitors to their established category leaders in CPG:

The Honest Company

This baby-bath-and-body-care product company, focused on nontoxic, environmentally safe products, famously has the actress Jessica Alba as a co-founder. The company started as online-only with monthly subscriptions, but moved offline into big chains like Whole Foods and Target. As result of this diversification, 30 percent of the Honest Company's revenue came from sales in brick-and-mortar chains, 42 percent from recurring monthly subscription, and the remaining 28 percent from other e-commerce sales. In 2015, The Honest Company raised $100 million at a reported $1.7 billion valuation and in 2016, was rumored to be pursuing both the path of an IPO, as well as an acquisition by an established Consumer Packaged Goods player.

The Honest Company expanded on the initial subscription model by diversifying into brick and mortar and e-commerce sales.

Dollar Shave Club

Founded in 2011, Dollar Shave Club rose to fame with their infamous "Our Blades Are F***ing Great" online video that went viral, with over 23 million views on YouTube. The company has become much more than just a funny video. External estimates put the company at over

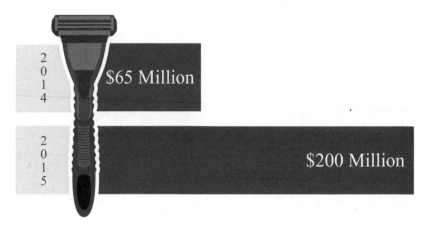

Dollar Shave Club continues to grow, more than tripling their earnings from 2014 to 2015.

$200 million in sales for 2015, triple the $65 million that the company publicly generated in 2014 from their 2 million members. Even more impressive, however, the company claimed in July 2015 to have passed Schick, becoming the #2 razor cartridge maker in the U.S. with over 16 percent volume share of cartridges. This growth led to their $1 billion acquisition by Unilever in July 2016.

Just about every big company that is now dealing with a major competitive threat from subscription commerce has had the opportunity to respond differently. To use Scott Lenet's words that started this chapter, they each had the opportunity to "see the future of their industry before it happened"– they just chose not to. Big companies decided that Subscription commerce was merely going to be a new retail channel and possibly a marketing channel for distributing product samples. Investors had a different view. David Pakman, the investor who led the Series A and B funding round for Dollar Shave, said after the acquisition by Unilever that: "To us [Venrock], we didn't see DSC as an 'e-commerce' company, but instead as a model for new full-stack consumer products companies."

In the tech world, the term full-stack originally referred to a developer that could code both the front-end and back-end of an application. What Pakman is referring to is the re-application of the term to describe a full-stack startup. In this case, a full-stack startup is a company like Dollar Shave Club that has a complete, end-to-end product that bypasses incumbents and other competitors.

Winning in this full-stack world actually requires a brand to change relationships with customers, day-to-day operations, analytical metrics and business models. It does not mean companies can just put a monthly price on a product, ship it, and complete the transaction. By refusing to change, many big brands missed the opportunity to combat emerging challengers, which are powered by customer preference data and built upon a new marketing model for direct customer acquisition. In the process, they also missed an opportunity that goes beyond channel acceleration or diversification. Subscription is actually a Trojan Horse for a new, direct and service-based relationship with the consumer and all the monetary opportunities that unlocks.

By refusing to change, big brands miss the opportunity to combat emerging challengers.

It did not have to be this way for any of those big companies – they could have transformed their business models to embrace this opportunity. Well before Dollar Shave Club, Ipsy or The Honest Company became household brands, the trend of subscription commerce was starting. During 2011 and 2012, $300 million in venture capital funding went into 50 subscription commerce startups across a wide range of industries. The inflow of capital only continued, demonstrated by $1.15 billion invested in subscription commerce by 2014, resulting in over

2,000 subscription box services. Subscription commerce emerged quickly, but it was easy to see it coming if you knew what you were looking for. There is nothing to indicate the change is over either. The internet – and thus e-commerce – has so deeply impacted the economics of business that it is only a matter of time before other categories are dramatically changed by the rise of Digitally Native Vertical Brands.

ABILITY TO SEE THE FUTURE

"He not busy being born is busy dying. That which is high-flying today might crash tomorrow. Always be looking in the rearview mirror, especially in tech, where everybody has the tools and the barrier to entry is low." —Bob Lefsetz, Lefsetz Letter

The concept of Market Intelligence is the ability to see the future of your industry before it happens. In the tradition of Cassandra from Greek mythology, it is the ability for companies to have the gift of prophecy for their business. With the right radar, CPG leaders would have recognized that companies like Birchbox were more likely to become emerging competitors than long-term strategic partners. By paying attention to this market intelligence, these brands would have gained a serious competitive advantage in understanding the future of their industry, the importance of subscription services and how they could increase their odds in this new market.

If a company is able to predict the turn, it gives them the ability to act from a position of strength. Intuit is a company that has followed this philosophy to guide their company strategy and transition in advance of an inevitable change. After selling two of its largest acquisitions – Intuit Financial Services and Intuit Health – the company set out to reinvent what its brand means to small-business owners. The company rallied behind a simple mission: "To be the operating system behind small business success and to do the nations' taxes in the U.S. and Canada." By practicing market intelligence, Intuit recognized that an industry-wide shift in business was happening from legacy desktop software to cloud platforms. Financially for Intuit this meant a move from one-time purchases and long upgrade cycles of desktop software to recurring revenue from cloud platforms where market share could be captured exponentially. Intuit realized this industry shift could either be to their benefit or to their detriment. With the challenge from their CEO to act like a "30-year-old startup," Intuit set the goal to shift 73 percent of its revenue from desktop to recurring subscription over a three-year period. To kickstart this transition, the company made 10 startup acquisitions in late 2013 through early 2014, more than the past five years combined. These acquisitions brought both the technology and the human talent that would allow Intuit to win in the high stakes game being played by cloud-first challengers.

BREADTH AND DEPTH

"Frankly, I'm more concerned about two guys in a garage."
—Jeff Bezos, CEO, Amazon

Big companies gain foresight by acting like venture capitalists when they engage with the startup community. Like any company, venture capitalists have a funnel – a pipeline of startups that are pitching them for investment. Venture Capitalists intentionally make this funnel as wide as possible at the top and, in most cases, as narrow as possible at the bottom (i.e., they only invest in a handful of companies each year despite seeing thousands of pitches). The reason they keep the funnel wide at the top is that they want to develop their view of the future by asking the questions: Where is an industry headed? What are the inefficiencies in the current market? What startups have the chance to become the dominant market leader with the right execution? The evaluation of startups and the market's climate inform their market intelligence, their view on how and when the future will happen. Informed market intelligence is how a venture capital firm like First Round Capital is able to be confident enough in the future to invest $500,000 into Uber at their seed round of funding. At that time, Uber was worth $4 million and its only product offering was an on-demand black car service that cost 1.5 times more than a taxi. First Round Capital invested not in where the market was then, but where the market was going tomorrow. Investors develop this future market intelligence by combining a breadth and depth of knowledge gained through their investment funnel; big companies can replicate this model to cultivate their own market intelligence.

Venture capitalists gain a breadth of knowledge from looking at thousands of companies that pitch them every year for investment. As deals come into their funnel, investors develop what is called pattern recognition around a certain space or industry. In its simplest form, pattern recognition is about looking at a wide data set and pulling lessons of what worked or did not work from those. For instance, venture capitalists note when multiple entrepreneurs launch startups in a certain amount of time around a variation of a similar business model. This is indicative of a broader pattern that can often be connected to a

Pattern recognition is looking at a wide data set and pulling lessons of what did or did not work.

theme playing out in the marketplace. Another leg of pattern recognition is looking at past behavior as an indicator of the future. An investor will look at past investments to glean what went right and wrong with those companies. They will then apply that world-view to current investment opportunities. In this sense, investors are using pattern recognition to shape their opinion on which startup has the best odds to be the market winner. Blue Chips are able to use this same approach around breadth of knowledge to build their pattern recognition around market trends. Building proper breadth requires going beyond a core category. Big companies need to meet not only with companies doing interesting things in their direct industry, but in adjacent industries, as well. This broad approach allows a company to use pattern recognition to connect the dots around an emerging innovation back into their core business.

Depth of knowledge builds upon the breadth and takes it a step further. When a venture capitalist finds a startup that is interesting, they start due diligence. This is the act of moving a startup down their funnel, going more in-depth to see if they are fit for investment. Most investors will pursue due diligence with fewer than five out of every 100 companies they meet. This is because due diligence is time-consuming and goes further than a simple one-hour pitch meeting. Investors use due diligence to develop a deeper understanding of industry trends, but also how companies in the market differentiate themselves from competitors. For instance, one part of due diligence often involves uncovering the customer value proposition by interviewing current customers (or potential customers) about the startup's solution and the problem it is solving. An investor might dig into the startup's business model to understand what it takes to run the business, acquire new customers, etc. Investors will even spend significant time with the management team, determining if they have the right background and skillsets to solve the market opportunity. They are looking to make a bet on both the jockey (the team at the startup) and the horse (the market/problem they are solving). On the other hand, big companies might go through true "due diligence" when exploring a potential acquisition, investment or even a partnership; it's important the big companies, like investors, spend more time with startups to build a depth of knowledge. Whenever a big company is looking at an emerging innovation like Subscription Commerce, there is significant value in them spending time not only with the startup, but also with their investors and even their customers. Doing so allows big companies to develop an opinion that is based on learning, not just on gut instinct. More importantly, it allows the company to develop a view on the market opportunity and what the company's appropriate approach should be.

A way to simultaneously build breadth and depth of knowledge is through growing relationships with the venture capital industry. While VCs serve as the inspiration for this market intelligence approach, they are also practitioners from whom big companies can learn a tremendous amount. After all, every venture capitalist will likely meet with close to 1,000 startups over the course of the year. Each relationship with an investor extends a company's personal market intelligence by a considerable magnitude. Although venture capitalists are funding and investing in many potential industry disruptors, they are also investing in plenty of portfolio companies where the livelihood of that business depends on either partnerships or selling to big companies. There is a strong motivating factor for those investors to build relationships with big companies, as many investors actually tout their industry relationships as a differentiator to startups. The relationships can be a win-win where each side has a positive motivating factor. Business leaders should embrace this mutual interest and use it to amplify their market knowledge in breadth and depth.

STARTUPS ARE THE CANARY IN THE COAL MINE

"The best time to repair the roof is when the sun is shining."
—Brad Smith, CEO of Intuit

For Blue Chips, the implications of breadth and depth are that startups can be the canary in the coal mine around emerging business models and consumers trends. A canary in a coal mine is an advanced warning of some danger. The metaphor originates from the times when miners used to carry caged canaries while at work; if there was any methane or carbon monoxide in the mine, the canary would die before the levels of the gas reached

those hazardous to humans. Startups can be that same early warning of danger for big brands.

Going back to subscription commerce, the very fact that investors were putting $300 million into 50+ startups in this space signaled a market trend. Although some very smart people believed subscription commerce was going to be a disruptive trend with major potential, most big companies did not think of it this way. They did not take a step back and analyze why subscription commerce was an emerging business model and how they could apply it to their own. Instead, they looked at the one or two startups in their industry that were launched around subscription commerce and made the decision in their minds if it was a good business or a bad business. They forgot to carry their cages with them.

OUTSIDERS OR DISRUPTORS

Venture capitalist Fred Wilson, a Managing Partner at Union Square Ventures, makes his living trying to identify the future and invest in the pioneers. In addition to being an early investor in companies like Twitter, Kik and SoundCloud, he is also the author of the widely read blog AVC. com. In one of his blog posts, Wilson shared the way he thinks about the concept of change, both as he evaluates potential investments and as he considers the impact on his existing portfolio:

> *"The question I always try to ask myself about new entrants in a market is "are they stupid or do they actually know something we don't?" Or said another way, are they outsiders or are they disruptors?"* [2]

The concept of gaining market intelligence through breadth and depth of knowledge is how big companies can make this same assessment about startups, by figuring out if they are outsiders or disruptors. After all, there is a downside to pattern recognition and assuming something will follow the same path as before. When a company is an expert in an industry, it is incredibly easy

Underestimating a disruptor is possibly the most dangerous behavior in business.

to quickly dismiss any startup as an outsider that does not understand the complexities of that particular market. Underestimating a disruptor is possibly the most dangerous behavior in business. Unfortunately for big companies, it happens to be a dangerous behavior that has played out several times. In fact, history is filled with companies that underestimated technologies, startups, and even other big companies that appeared to be outsiders instead of disruptors.

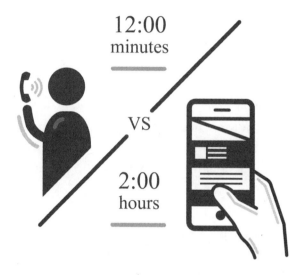

The evolution of the mobile phone resulted in a drastic drop in actual time spent making phone calls. With a miniature computer in their hands, consumer behavior shifted from talking to texting and browsing.

Consider big companies that saw Apple as just an outsider trying to move into mobile phones. Steve Ballmer, Microsoft's CEO in 2007, famously said, "There's no chance that the iPhone is going to get any significant market." Palm's CEO Ed Colligan, speaking as a true "insider" said in 2006, "We've learned and struggled for a few years here figuring out how to make a decent phone . . . PC guys are not going to just figure this out. They're not going to just walk in." The issue for Palm and others is that Apple was not trying to build a "decent phone." Today, the average iPhone user spends over two hours a day on their device but only 12 minutes of that is making phone calls. Insiders felt people wanted a better phone. Steve Jobs, the CEO of Apple, realized people wanted a computer in their pocket.

Speaking of insiders missing the mark in "phones," AT&T underestimated the market potential of the very cell phone that Apple ultimately went on to dominate. In 1980, AT&T commissioned McKinsey & Company – whose Bell Labs had invented the technology behind cell phones – to forecast cell phone penetration in the U.S. by 2000. McKinsey predicted that in the next 20 years, cell phones would only reach a total of 900,000 subscribers. Unfortunately for AT&T, this prediction completely misrepresented cell phones as an outsider, when in fact they were a disruptor. The prediction was actually exceeded less than seven years later, in 1987, with 1.2 million subscribers in the U.S. and made up only 1 percent of the actual figure of 109 million cell phone subscribers in 2000.

On the startup side, big companies have repeatedly considered the startups to be an outsider that does not have a clue about their consumers, instead of an innovative disruptor. In an interview with the magazine *Fast Company*, the EVP of Product Operations at the Four Seasons said, "Our guests don't want the Airbnb feel and scent . . . our level of service is different, more sophisticated, detailed, and skillful." Yet head over to Airbnb and you can find several "sophisticated" properties costing nearly $10,000 per night including a private chateau in France and a 12-acre estate in San Francisco where Beyoncé and Jay Z stayed during Super Bowl 50. With a breadth of offerings, Airbnb booked over 37 million nights in 2014; a report by Barclays projects that by 2017, the company will be booking more rooms than the world's largest hotel chains (including the Four Seasons).

TAM IS THE SIZE OF THE POT

"Sizing the market for a disruptor based on an incumbent's market is like sizing the car industry off how many horses there were in 1910."

—Aaron Levie, CEO & Founder, Box[3]

In 1920, America had more than 25 million horses and mules. While they were used for transportation, most were mainly used for farm work. The invention of the automobile for transportation and the tractor for farm work meant the 1920s were the last great decade for the usefulness of these animals. By the 1960s, the numbers of these work animals settled to where they remain today – at about one-tenth of the levels in 1920. Meanwhile, in modern times, there are 4.5 million tractors and over 250 million cars in the U.S. As Aaron eloquently points out, the impact of the automobile disruption could never have been predicted by counting the "technology" it disrupted.

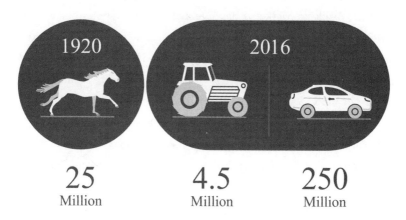

1920	2016
25 Million	4.5 Million 250 Million

The tractor and automobile disruption could not be predicted simply by counting the "technology" it disrupted.

The reason a big company should aspire to build market intelligence through working with startups is so they can avoid metaphorically "counting horses." The issue is that for many companies, they have spent decades focusing on the "share of horses." Business has been about established competitors and battle for market share forever; think Coke vs. Pepsi or Old Spice vs. Axe where one percent of market share might be worth hundreds of millions of dollars. The flaw with that thinking in today's digital world is that the market share of tomorrow will look like the market share of today. As the incumbent, you cannot just look at the industry you are in and assume that is where it is going to be decades from now. It's important to realize that innovation will change the market, whether you want it to or not.

Part of market intelligence is thinking about the Total Available Market (or TAM for short). TAM is venture speak for the market size that Aaron Levie mentions above. TAM is thinking about the maximum market where a startup could potentially compete. Or said another way, Total Available Market is the potential size of the pot you are playing for. Take Uber for instance. Is Uber just competing in the taxi and limousine market that is historically worth $100 billion? Is Uber actually competing in the car rental industry, as well (a $27 billion industry in the U.S.)? Could Uber reach a point in terms of price and convenience that it becomes a preferable alternative to owning a car ($730 billion in cars are sold each year)? None of these even account for the moves that Uber has started to make into logistics and same-day delivery. Total Available Market paints a picture of what is possible tomorrow, not just what is real today. Looking at your industry through the lens of TAM leads to an entirely new way of thinking about your business and is a springboard that gives permission to behave very, very differently as company.

As Blue Chips work with startups through investment, acquisition or partnership, the overarching umbrella benefit is the market intelligence that helps a company to see into the future. They need to approach these activities with the mindset of the venture capitalist, thinking about the potential of where something could go tomorrow, not just where it is today. In high stakes business, Blue Chips need to ask themselves a few key questions to build their market intelligence:

- **What business is your company in today / tomorrow?**
  This is not about analyzing the current competitors or even the category of your business. Instead, it is about answering the high order question of what you help your customers to do in their lives. Ford is not in the car business, they are in the mobility business. Nike is not in the sneaker business, they are in the athletic performance business. And Facebook is in the business of sharing life moments – the very business that Kodak should have moved into.

- **What is Total Available Market of these new opportunities?**
  For many Blue Chips, disruption is perceived as a threat when it should actually be reframed as an opportunity. With a mindset of TAM, these new opportunities allow a company to focus on growth instead of simply fighting over market share.

- **What is the approach forward to realize these opportunities?**
  As mentioned in the beginning of this chapter, Blue Chips have been able to reach their dominant position today because of stability. While the market is changing, incumbents should use this leadership position as a platform to build share rather than just defend it. The following chapters will showcase the various options that a Blue Chip might leverage to take advantage of these opportunities.

The market intelligence gained answering these questions will allow Blue Chips to develop a sense of how and when the future will happen in your industry – before it actually happens. This obviously will not guarantee victory in high stakes business, but it puts you in the position where the odds are vastly in your favor. It gives a your company the advantage to predict the turn.

KEY TAKEAWAYS

- Market Intelligence is developing a sense of how and when the future will happen in a given industry, while using breadth and depth of knowledge gained through frequent engagement with startups.

- Innovators attacking an existing market can be classified as either outsiders or disruptors. Established companies must be cautious to not quickly dismiss an innovator as outsider that does not understand the industry. Use Market Intelligence to determine if they "know something that you don't."

- Do not become narrowly focused on your company's share of today's market. Broaden the view to look at the Total Available Market that is likely the target for disruptors entering the market.

- Good pattern recognition is an unfair competitive advantage that saves you time and gives your company a head start.

THE TURN

NatureBox

Gautam Gupta has been recognized as one of Inc. Magazine's "30 Under 30 Best and Brightest Entrepreneurs" for his work as Co-Founder and CEO of NatureBox – a direct-to-consumer snack company that makes smart, delicious snacking easy. Launched in 2012, NatureBox has quickly become one of America's fastest-growing food brands by leveraging real-time consumer data to drive innovation and bring new products to market every month. Having started his career on the Big Company side, Gautam shares his view on how NatureBox can be an inspiration to Blue Chips when it comes to innovation.

Gautam Gupta:

The stats in the packaged goods industry paint an urgent picture of change. Ninety of the top 100 brands are losing market share, in fact the top 25 have lost $19B in market share over the past seven years. Even the brands that are growing are lagging their category average growth rate, which means that even if you're in a growth category, you're struggling. Look to your own consumption, how many brands do you buy today that simply didn't exist ten years ago? For me, the change is clear but surprising. After all, Big Companies know so much about their customers, they have armies of consumer insights experts and stockpiles of data. My own experience inside P&G's market knowledge group taught me that there is no shortage of data or insights, but the real challenge rests in turning the ship. I believe that the challenge facing the CPG industry today is not our understanding of the consumer but our ability to execute on this. As the consumer world evolves, you must question whether an 18-to-24 month innovation cycle is justified. Big Companies can't afford to stick innovation into a never-ending stage gate process and be left playing from behind.

NatureBox has taken a different approach, one focused on trial and error. In Silicon Valley there is a startup mantra to "fail fast," which is accompanied by strongly differing views on the value of failure. However, whether or not you see value in failure, the emphasis on speed is what is most important. Consumer trends are changing at a rapid pace; the ability to move quickly is now a competitive advantage. In our model, we aim to learn fast which includes winning and failing more than anyone else. We've built a system that minimized the cost and risk associated with failure so that we can afford to take more bets. In the context of a poker game, we get to see the flop every time without posting blinds.

> ## The emphasis on speed is what is most important.

Over the past four years, NatureBox has developed and launched over 300 products with a development cycle of 10 to 14 weeks. Unlike most brands, instead of focusing on one product line, we focus on a wide array of products that the consumer can easily switch between. We want you to be loyal to our brand but we're going to earn that loyalty through an ever-changing assortment of products at a great value. Our product launches are all tests, minimizing our expenses until enough data can be gathered to place a product squarely in the win or loss column. Beyond our products, we're building technology that intelligently promotes our products to individual customers based on their taste preferences and the ability for our customers to vote on products as they move through our development pipeline. This approach of rapid innovation and testing only works if you can move quickly. Four years into NatureBox, here is what we have learned to increase our tempo:

Create a space to experiment.   Often the most significant delay to launch timing in CPG is caused by our retail partners' reset schedule. Getting up to bat once-a-year or twice-a-year simply isn't enough. At NatureBox, this experiment space is our direct-to-consumer business where we own the relationship with the customer. This channel allows us to create and change the customer experience, which we did on nearly a daily basis in 2015. We are able to launch products at any time and within a few weeks; we have enough data to determine the success or failure of the launch. Perhaps the DTC channel fills that need for your company or perhaps a regional retail chain might.

Determine the one metric that defines success.   We are a company that aspires to track everything and yet, one of our key insights is to not drown in data. We collect ratings, reviews, purchase history, social media comments, and the list goes on but we've found one metric to measure product success. We think this metric is aligned with our primary objective of retention and, most importantly, drives action. How you define the metric itself doesn't matter, but the simplicity of one number has reduced the unnecessary debate and increased our decision-making speed.

Re-think the process with timelines in mind.   When we began NatureBox, one of the operational challenges we faced in developing new products so quickly, was that the lead time on packaging was often three months or more. This took us down a path of looking at every step in getting a product to market and optimizing for time. We quickly discovered ways to shrink the packaging lead-time as well as sequence our process in such a way that minimized bottlenecks. We even start our product development process with a cross functional approval meeting which green lights the project from the beginning – avoiding re-work and delays as we get closer to launch. The lesson we learned was to not let perfect be the enemy of good. At every step in the process we had to make trade offs for speed but often those did not impact the success of the test.

Adopt a new view on capabilities and resources.   Big Companies have become aggregators of capabilities and in the pursuit of incremental profit, that approach has produced great return. However, the next generation of brands is increasingly looking to simplify their operating models by outsourcing production and fulfillment, partner with agencies, and use third-party software. NatureBox.com operates across dozens of servers, none of which we own. To get new businesses off the ground, often it is easier and faster to do things outside of the company's infrastructure. Even at NatureBox, we look for ways to leverage outside technology and have even stood up test sites outside of our core infrastructure, knowing that we can learn faster that way without distracting our core team.

By going direct-to-consumer, we feel that we have created a platform for innovation. Our business is built on experimentation that aims to continuously improve the customer experience. Over a few years of trial by fire, we've found ways to further accelerate our business and often those are by looking at our objective, process, and resources in a new way.

CHAPTER 3

INNOVATION-DRIVEN ACQUISITION

"You can fight the [end of car ownership], and that will probably not turn out well. Or you can acknowledge that this is happening. This is real, serious, and going to change your world."

—John Zimmer, President and co-founder, Lyft at Los Angeles Auto Show, November 2015

AS 2016 STARTED, unprecedented changes confronted the world's automakers and struck the very core of their industry. Unlike so many others, the automaker industry had remained nearly constant for the past 100 years – at least when it came to the fundamental business model of car ownership.

No place was that sense of ownership stronger than with teenagers. The rite of passage for a teenager to get their driver's license became a symbol of freedom, of their coming adulthood. However, over the last decade, a change had started to occur. For starters, young people aged 16 to 34 began to drive less – to the tune of 23 percent fewer miles on average in 2009 than in 2001. Corresponding to that, "69 percent of 19-year-olds had licenses in 2014, compared to 87.3 percent in 1983, a 21-percent decrease."[1] This resulted in the lowest number of 16-year-olds ever to get their drivers licenses that year. The rise of social networking and the mobile phone were two catalysts of this change. Cars used to be the sole source of freedom for teenagers to connect with their friends. But today, Facebook and the iPhone provide a similar sense of freedom. In fact, a study conducted by researchers at the University of Michigan discovered that "a higher proportion of internet users was associated with a lower licensure rate," which they found to be "consistent with the hypothesis that access to virtual contact reduces the need for actual contact among young people." Said another way, the News Feed became a replacement for Drivers Ed.

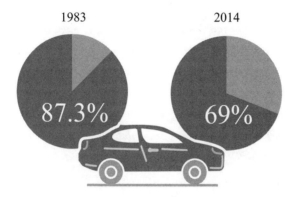

1983   2014

87.3%   69%

The rate of 19-year-old drivers has decreased 18.3% since 1983.

As if this fundamental consumer change were not challenging enough, Big Auto has also had to face the entry of Silicon Valley into their industry. Every week seems to bring a new headline of Uber and its ever-inflating $60+ billion-dollar valuation. Tesla and its efforts to disrupt car dealerships by selling direct. Google's efforts to build the world's first truly self-driving car. These outsiders are not a repeat of the Detroit vs. Japan battle of the 1990s, but instead it's a fundamental business challenge to automakers around the world.

The automakers faced a study of contrast. On one hand, fundamental changes were taking place around mobility. Yet, at the same time, the industry had records sales in Q4 2015. With this as a backdrop, 2016 saw several of the Big Auto companies – at least those wanting to avoid their own Kodak moment – take the bold first steps in a "pivot" toward being Mobility companies. In the startup world, "pivot" is a word that is sometimes tossed around without a clear meaning. Steve Blank, who is credited with launching the lean startup movement with his book *Four Steps to the Epiphany*, attempted to put clear boundaries around the word by writing that:

> "A pivot is not just changing the product. A pivot can change any of nine different things in your business model. A pivot may mean you changed your customer segment, your channel, revenue model/pricing, resources, activities, costs, partners, customer acquisition – lots of other things than just the product. A pivot is defined as a substantive change to one or more of the 9 business model canvas components."[2]

The pivot in Detroit began in January 2016 with major announcements from both Ford Motor Company and General Motors. The automakers announced a move from being just auto manufacturers to becoming full-service mobility companies that are better able to compete against disruptors like Uber, Tesla and Google.

At Ford Motor Company, the "blue oval" announced the launch of Ford-Pass, a platform that reimagines the relationship between automaker and consumer. FordPass focuses on the Consumer Experience and bridging a gap between physical and digital. This platform would give Ford the ability to interact with a consumer every day versus every few years when they buy or lease a new car. To launch this new platform, Ford took the approach of partnership with startups. They announced partnerships with companies like ParkWhiz – startups that allowed Ford to offer new mobility solutions like advanced parking reservations without building the functionality from scratch. When talking about the launch of FordPass, Ford's CEO Mark Fields commented:

> *"The point is that it's not moving from an old business to a new business. It's just moving to a bigger business as we expand the business model from number of units sold to number of units sold plus vehicle miles traveled."*

Across town, General Motors took a slightly different approach. Instead of just partnering with startups, GM went the financial route leveraging both investment and acquisition in its move toward transforming into a mobility company. In the first few months of 2016, GM announced that it exchanged less than 5 percent of its market capitalization (and less than 10 percent of its cash) in the following deals:

- On January 4, 2016, GM announced a $500 million investment in Lyft, the ride-hailing startup that in its battle with Uber was providing 7 million rides per month, across more than 190 cities in the United States. The investment valued Lyft at $5.5 billion, which meant GM would own just under 10 percent of the company.

- In mid-January, GM followed up by acquiring Sidecar, the ride-hailing pioneer that owned one of the patents that is essential intellectual property behind ride-sharing. The acquisition was also one of talent, with GM bringing on board around 20 employees from the Sidecar team (though co-founder and Chief Technology Officer Jahan Khanna left only one month after the purchase to join Uber). This acquisition coincided with its launch of Maven, a new global car-sharing service in Ann Arbor, Chicago, Denver and New York City.

- In what might be the biggest splash, GM bought Cruise Automation, a three-year-old Silicon Valley startup that specializes in autonomous vehicle technology. While not confirmed initially, the rumored acquisition price was over $1 billion in a mix of cash and GM stock.

These moves were not the first by the big automakers to move into mobility via investment or acquisition. Fontinalis Partners, which was co-founded by Bill Ford, has been "investing in the future of mobility" since 2009. The GM Venture Fund has been around since 2010. In 2014, Daimler AG acquired German ridesharing apps RideScout and mytaxi. Nokia created its Connected Car venture fund in 2014. In addition, BMW has been an active investor through their BMW i Incubator and corporate venture capital group, BMW i Ventures, which has bought stakes in Moovit (multi-modal app), JustPark (parking reservations) and Zirx (valet parking/on-demand services). BMW's Board Member for R&D, Klaus Froehlich, sees mobility players like Uber and TrueCar as the "new intermediaries" and said that BMW's task is "to preserve our business model without surrendering it to an internet player. Otherwise we will end up as the Foxconn for a company like Apple, delivering only the metal bodies for them."[3]

Reinforcing the point made by Froehlich is Marc Andreessen's famous quote, "Software is eating the world." In the *Wall Street Journal* article that sparked this saying, Andreessen went on to state that, "More and more major businesses and industries are being run on software and delivered as online services – from movies to agriculture to national defense. Many of the winners are Silicon Valley–style entrepreneurial technology companies that are invading and overturning established industry structures." With connected cars, autonomous driving, and electric vehicles, the automotive industry is one of the next industries where software will threaten, if not overturn, the establishment. What is the cost of falling behind in the transformation of the auto industry into software companies? Big companies who are unable to transform into software companies risk playing in a low-margin commoditized hardware game. History has shown that it's better to be Microsoft than to make Gateway personal computers.

This is the reason that General Motors and the other auto manufacturers are making the move toward mobility companies. The words of GM President Daniel Ammann after the acquisition of Cruise perfectly sum it up:

> *"We're seeing significant changes in the industry and we're taking very assertive actions to put our company at the forefront. We're following and moving with our customers. We want to be able to serve them in whatever way they want their car-based transportation."*

BIGCO BUYING NEWCO

"I think we're in the middle of a huge business paradigm shift. Legacy companies have so much invested in the status quo way of doing things that they have a hard time arranging their assets in this new way. The only way they're going to survive is by buying these new companies." —Robin Chase, Co-Founder, ZipCar[4]

The financial path that General Motors went down is the one that is often the first reaction that brands have when they encounter startups. After you look at the balance sheets of these big companies, it is easy to understand why. These are companies that are generating hundreds of millions of dollars in profits and control both marketing and R&D budgets that are often that size or larger. Therefore, the concept of investing several million dollars in a startup (covered in the next chapter) or even buying them for a multiple of that is not really intimidating.

The appeal is further increased when looking at the success stories – or at least the stories that could have been. It is not uncommon when a big company is starting work with a startup to hear "what if" comments around "what if they become the next Google?" There are also the "if only" stories that serve as inspiration, such as in 2000 when Reed Hastings approached former Blockbuster CEO John Antioco and tried to sell his fledging startup Netflix for $50 million. Antioco, thinking that it was a "very small niche business," ended the negotiations and obviously did not buy Netflix. Eight years later, Blockbuster's new CEO Jim Keyes still did not regret the decision, as he told Motley Fool that, "Neither RedBox nor Netflix are even on the radar screen in terms of competition. It's more Walmart and Apple."[5] Fast-forward another eight years to today, Blockbuster is bankrupt while Netflix has a market cap of over $45 billion.

However, this short-sighted worldview is dangerous thinking for any company if it is not based on sound strategic rationale. Hubris and conformational bias are the enemy of businesses big and small. A solid business cannot be built on "what if" and "if only." Any sort of financial involvement with another company, particularly a startup, has serious implications that cannot be underestimated, no matter the size of the check.

With that said, becoming involved in a startup through financial means can be one of the most beneficial ways for a company to drive innovation and disruption. And, if done correctly with aligned incentives, it can be tremendously rewarding for all parties involved. Let's start with Acquisition, which involves purchasing all of a startup's assets including their product, technology, intellectual property and employees.

INNOVATION-DRIVEN ACQUISITION

To borrow terminology from the world of poker, making an acquisition of a startup is a company "going all-in." Every Fortune 500 has experiences with Mergers & Acquisitions (commonly referred to as M&A) so I'm not referring to acquisitions in that broad sense. Instead, this is about an acquisition of a startup with the strategic intent to bring a company into new markets or introduce disruptive technologies. Let's call it innovation-driven acquisition; think more along the lines of General Motors buying Cruise and Sidecar instead of Procter & Gamble buying Gillette. The technology industry is distinctive from other industries because the pace of innovation moves faster than many traditional businesses. As a result, M&A can be a tool to solve time-to-market issues much quicker than internal product development. Building upon that, innovation-driven acquisition generally falls in three categories:

CORE Acquisitions that bring innovation to existing products and business models. This often includes optimizing existing products for existing customers.

ADJACENT Acquisitions that bring innovation where a corporation enters a new market that is adjacent to their current – often expanding from existing businesses into "new to the company" businesses.

EMERGENT Acquisitions that bring innovation through disruptive products, technologies or business models. This means acquiring breakthroughs where a company enters a new market, with new products for new customers.

Acquisition behaviors are seen frequently in the halls of Big Tech companies. Google, for instance, hired 221 startup founders through acquisitions it made between 2006 and 2014. Microsoft has completed more than 175 M&A deals in its history. Additionally, for a company that has only been around for a decade, Twitter has already closed more than 35 acquisitions. Yet, one of the more inspiring examples is Facebook. Over its history Facebook has made over 50 acquisitions, mostly for talent during its early hyper-growth years where it subsequently shut down the products purchased (like

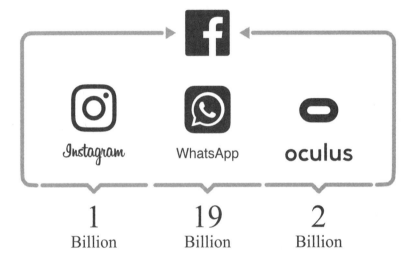

Facebook has expanded its digital empire by acquiring companies that compete for mindshare in their audience, instead of acquiring similar services to what Facebook already offers.

FriendFeed and HotPotato). However, since going public, Facebook has changed its acquisition strategy, focusing on purchasing companies that are competing for the mindshare and engagement of its audience. This strategy has led them into adjacent markets beyond just "social networking" including photo-sharing (Instagram for $1 billion), mobile instant messaging (WhatsApp for $19 billion), and virtual reality (Oculus

VR for $2 billion). The result: Facebook has built a technology "house of brands," the very strategy that built the great consumer packaged goods companies like P&G, Unilever, and Nestlé. In contrast to a conglomerate like GE with disparate businesses, the Facebook house of brands revolves around their core revenue model of advertising. Ninety-seven percent of Facebook's revenue comes from advertising, which in turn comes from the "eyeballs" of their 1.6 billion users. The acquisitions of Instagram, WhatsApp, and Oculus VR were about Facebook diversifying beyond social networking into adjacent markets that were related to their core business. Ultimately they are about the vision of the company's founder to make Facebook and the internet inseparable. As Redef wrote, if they are successful, "Facebook will own attention infrastructure, communications infrastructure (WhatsApp, Messenger), your relationships and family/friend-trees (Facebook's social graph), online identities (Facebook log-in), online experiences (virtual reality) and on and on. Whatever you do and however you experience it, Facebook powers, delivers and manages your online activities."

"PROTECT THIS HOUSE"

Like many great entrepreneurs, Kevin Plank started with a desire to solve a personal pain point. As special teams captain on the University of Maryland football team, Plank was frustrated that the cotton t-shirts that his team wore underneath their pads were always soaked and heavy with sweat. With the desire to make something better, Plank set out to find a shirt that would stay light and dry even after the toughest workout. While the lore of Silicon Valley is to start your company in a garage, Kevin Plank started Under Armour at the age of 23 in his grandmother's basement. Plank built his first prototype with a fabric found in New York's garment district, maxed out his credit cards to the tune of

$40,000, and gave the samples to his Maryland teammates and friends who had gone on to play in the NFL. Their positive feedback fueled the birth of the performance apparel industry, an entirely new category of moisture-wicking apparel that keeps athletes cool, dry and light. Two decades later, Under Armour is a business with over $4 billion in annual revenue a five-year compound annual growth rate of 29.5 percent. While Nike is still six times the size of Under Armour, just five years ago they were twelve times larger and Under Armour recently passed Adidas to become the second largest sportswear brand in the U.S.

However, Under Armour realizes that innovation is not a one-time thing and they relish the opportunity to challenge industry norms. Today, the company is using the power of acquisitions to broaden its business in this new digital economy, using its heritage as a springboard. In 2013, Under Armour started to lay the groundwork for what would eventually become the Connected Fitness business. The journey started when the company spent $150 million on exercise app MapMyFitness in November 2013, then in February 2015 paid $475 million for calorie-counting app MyFitnessPal, and $85 million for European fitness app Endomondo. Totaling $700 million, the acquisitions cost Under Armour the equivalent of the company's last three years of pretax profit. But, the result is that Under Armour now controls the world's biggest digital fitness platform. They ended 2015 with 160 million registered users that logged eight billion meals and two billion activities over the course of the year. With 60+ million people logging on to one of its apps at least once a month, Under Armour has positioned itself at the epicenter of the consumer's active lifestyle.

In the company's 2015 Annual Report, Plank called out that Connected Fitness "is not a technology initiative. This is a digital transformation and therefore a business transformation for Under Armour." Plank went on to say that, "On the whiteboards in my office I have written in big, bright red letters – 'Don't forget to sell shirt and shoes.'" The power of Connected Fitness is that it allows Plank to sell more shirts by becoming part of the athlete's life, 24/7. From sleep and activity, to fitness and nutrition, Under Armour is individually interacting with consumers, turning their data into a call to action to support its mission to "make all athletes better."

DON'T LET THE TECH WAVE PASS YOU BY

The ability of corporations to create disruptive innovation internally has not kept up with the overall brisk pace of the technology industry. As a result, the largest and fastest growing category in the most recent PwC M&A Report is Transformational. In the PwC Survey, respondents reported an increase in transformational deals from 29 percent to 44 percent, and a corresponding decrease in absorption deals by similar amounts, from 40 percent to 29 percent. Transformational Deals are those that involve acquiring new markets, channels, products or operations in a way that is transformative to the fully integrated organization. Absorption Deals are those that involve acquiring and integrating similar companies as their own, such as industry competitors (also called consolidation). Transformational deals, like Under Armour with MapMyFitness, are clearly innovation-driven acquisition.

Under Armour is not alone in its efforts to acquire its way into digital expertise to avoid having the tech wave pass their company by. Other examples of innovation-driven acquisition by major corporations of earlier stage, venture-backed startups include:

- **Home Depot** bought Redbeacon, the home services marketplace, and BlackLocus, the data-driven pricing analytics startup. BlackLocus served as the founding base for the new "Home Depot Innovations Lab" in Austin, Texas.

- **Nordstrom** acquired the limited-time flash sales website HauteLook for $270 million and the men's shopping service Trunk Club for $350 million. Nordstrom also led an investment in Bonobos, the online e-tailer that makes better-fitting pants that are made-to-order via the company's website.

- **Monsanto**, the $15 billion agriculture company, bought The Climate Corporation for $930 million in October 2013.

- **Mars Pet Care** purchased Whistle, maker of a GPS location monitor and fitness tracking device for dogs for $119 million.

- **Fossil Group**, a $3.5 billion-a-year, global fashion-accessories brand that makes watches, leather goods, jewelry and sunglasses, bought wearable-technology maker Misfit for $260 million.[6]

In each of these examples, the acquirer was able to buy the would-be disruptors and infused digital DNA into their core business. For instance, Climate, which underwrites weather insurance for farmers, gave Monsanto the opportunity to sell more data and services to the farmers who already buy Monsanto's seed and chemicals. These startups have opened the eyes of their new parent companies to what it takes to survive in today's digital world through new business models, modern technology stacks, and emerging categories.

The other benefit of acquisition comes with acquiring talent, both to boost the current management ranks as well as bring future leaders on board. When Under Armour purchased MapMyFitness, it bought not only a great digital product and community, but also the digital talent that built the business. Robin Thurston, who co-founded MapMyFitness, joined Under Armour as Chief Digital Officer and for several years led its Austin, Texas, team with over 150 employees.

Related to the point of talent, acquisitions need to be about more than money. A Blue Chip must ask what unfair advantage do they bring in an acquisition. Cash is cheap and if a BigCo is just a checkbook, then they are saying they can operate a current business better than the management team that is in place. While unlocking value in this way was

> # A Blue Chip must ask what unfair advantage do they bring in an acquisition.

possible in legacy acquisitions, innovation-driven acquisitions requires something more. While it is cliché, acquisitions are about looking for opportunities where one plus one equals three. It is about finding ways where the resources of the acquirer can accelerate the efforts of the acquisition.

In high stakes business, innovation-driven acquisition is going all-in and making the bold bet for the future of the business. It is an opportunity to not only acquire new business models, but also new talent that will lead your company toward this future direction. Acquisition can serve as acceleration, offering an unique strategy for companies to solve a variety of challenges.

KEY TAKEAWAYS

- Innovation-driven acquisition of external startups can accelerate internal product development, go-to-market, and the speed/timing of both.

- Acquisitions of startups generally fall into three categories:
  CORE Optimizing existing products for existing customers,
  ADJACENT Expanding from existing businesses into "new to the company" businesses, and
  EMERGENT Entering a new market with new products for new customers.

- Companies are increasingly looking at acquisitions in the technology space to infuse digital DNA into their core businesses – both in terms of business models, as well as human talent.

- Big Companies need to consider what "industry" they play in and the potential ancillary markets. Under Armour recognized that just playing in fitness apparel limits its market size, while Connected Fitness provides a broader industry opportunity. Companies need to find innovation in the periphery and expose it with the incumbent scale and resources.

- Acquisitions need to be more about strategy than about money. A Blue Chip must ask what unfair advantage do they bring in an acquisition. Cash is cheap and if a BigCo is just a checkbook, then they are saying they can operate a current business better than the management team that is in place.

E.W. Scripps Co.

*Rich Boehne is chairman, president and CEO of
The E.W. Scripps Co., a Cincinnati-based broadcast and
digital media company founded in 1878. Boehne, a former
reporter, joined the Scripps corporate team as head of
investor relations when the company went public in 1988.
He took the helm when the company spun off its cable
networks in 2008, and he has led the effort to reinvent the
company several times since then.*
Rich Boehne:

At The E.W. Scripps Company, our strategy discussions are
guided by a restless insecurity and an acceptance that, practically
speaking, the media business is still relatively young and wildly
unpredictable.

Over our nearly 140-year history, the company has remade,
restructured and rebuilt itself many times, keeping up and, at least

so far, staying far enough ahead of technological developments to thrive and build value in the next season of media history.

We have owned newspapers, radio stations, broadcast television stations, cable television systems, cable networks, digital media and commerce brands, a large licensing division that owned the Peanuts characters and handled many others, television programming operations and a long list of other media-related ventures. Plus, we steward one spelling bee that each year captivates a national audience with its final rounds live on ESPN.

After having spun off our cable networks (including HGTV and The Food Network) in 2008 and our newspapers in 2015, we are today a leading operator of local television and digital brands and an aggressive investor in evolving digital brands – both video and audio.

We started these investments in early 2014 by acquiring Newsy, a five-year-old millennial video news service out of Columbia, Missouri, and launching it on dozens of over-the-top video platforms, including AppleTV, SlingTV and Roku. The following year, we bought the leading podcasting production and ad network, Midroll Media, in order to reach the affluent and largely younger audiences who love podcasts. And later, we bought the consumer podcast discovery platform Stitcher to complement it. Then we bought the vintage satire brand *Cracked* – which started in the 50s as a humor magazine competing with *MAD* but now has 20 million visitors to its website and another 20 million views of its YouTube videos each month.

These acquisitions add up to revenue that is a fraction of what we make in traditional television, which remains healthy and offers opportunities of its own. We made these digital investments as a way to reach new demographic groups and because we believe they can scale over time to become meaningful contributors. Perhaps they will eventually outpace our broadcast business; perhaps they will remain smaller players.

The only thing we fully accept as gospel truth is that the enterprise will look somewhat different to very different – again – in a few short years. The constant over our history is a commitment to public service journalism in whatever format best serves audiences. Everything else, particularly how it's delivered, is open to debate.

Today, Scripps is navigating one of the media industry's most relentless periods of evolution as the internet – a worldwide digital grid – becomes video's primary distribution platform. During the past 40 years, viewers have navigated and paid for their television consumption according to how they physically receive it – through a cable, over the air from broadcast towers or beamed down from satellites. As each of those distribution platforms becomes part of the overall digital grid, the distinctions between them are falling away. Viewers are selecting and customizing their own television packages based purely on what they want to watch – not forced to choose based on what's available on any one particular platform.

This could be the first time the media industry will reach some notion of a steady state; when the distribution channel will become ubiquitous and some of the pioneering technologies will be relegated to supporting niches.

Printing presses enabled "mass media" beginning in the late 1800s. Today it's the digital grid that can in a moment amass seven out of ten humans walking the earth and, at the same time, reach each one of them almost by name.

OPPORTUNITY? PERIL? IS THERE A DIFFERENCE?

We don't see a difference, at least not the way Scripps approaches its planning for the future. We recently turned to a more fluid and less balkanized system of planning, enlisting some of our best thinkers to develop broad future scenarios for the business. Cross-discipline groups were assembled and asked to project possible paths for the company "value drivers" – in many cases external forces – instead of looking simply at the future of its more traditional lines of business.

With the first phase complete, the work moves to finding business opportunities out of a realm of possibilities. The strategic planning process identifies a number of paths forward, so the next step is to ask what decisions the company needs to make today to create value longer term.

Scripps is a company of questioners – skeptical yet optimistic and always with an eye toward what's next. This culture has served us well for nearly a century and a half, and we expect it to help us thrive for at least the next 100 years.

CHAPTER 4

INVEST IN CHANGE

"Sometimes, incidentally, it's much easier in these transforming events to figure out the losers. You could have grasped the importance of the auto when it came along but still found it hard to pick companies that would make you money."

—Warren Buffett

WARREN BUFFETT and Marc Andreessen are two of the most influential business leaders of the late 20th century. However, beyond their business clout and being born less than 250 miles apart in the Midwest, their views tend to differ on many subjects including investing. Buffett once said that he does not invest in software businesses because he wants to invest in things that are not going to change. In an infamous *Fortune* article penned during the dot-com bubble of 1999–2000, Buffett explained, "The key to investing is not assessing how much an industry is going to affect society, or how much it will grow" but to examine two areas:

- The relatively limited longevity and defensibility of competitive advantage in tech (i.e., lack of a "moat");

- The difficulty of identifying the few winners in advance and being able to buy them at reasonable prices.[1]

Buffett's point, which he went on to describe, is that in times of monumental social change, there are more losers than there are winners. If you look at two of the transformative industries of the 20th century – the automobile and the airplane – today there are just a handful of manufacturers. Yet, there were over 1,800 automobile manufacturers in the United States from 1896 to 1930 when the industry was just being started. Of course, the clear loser in the transformative event of the automobile was the fact that horse ownership peaked in 1920.

"We invest on the side of change."   —Marc Andreessen

Marc Andreessen, the founder of Netscape and the venture capital firm Andreessen Horowitz, says he tries to invest in the other side of that – the change itself. As he said in an interview: "Nothing makes us happier than when something has been going for 30 or 40 years and we find a technology that will make that obsolete and the new thing captures all the value."

So who is right? The Oracle of Omaha who has been so successful in his investment activity at Berkshire Hathaway that he is annually the second or third richest man in the world? Or Andreessen, who has been dubbed "Tomorrow's Advanced Man" and one of the best technological minds of all time?

In a way, both are right. They just happen to be looking at two different sides of the same coin.

To explain why, let's start by defining "investing." For that, I'll turn again to the wise words of Buffett, who clearly knows a thing or two about it:

> *"The definition is simple but often forgotten: Investing is laying out money now to get more money back in the future – more money in real terms, after taking inflation into account."*

Investing in change, or what also might be called disruptive innovation, is difficult to predict. Andreessen takes the view that he wants to back the companies driving the change, while Buffett takes the other side of the coin and would rather invest in the ones who will survive the change. The similarity in their views is that they both recognize that technological innovation can, and most often will, have dramatic impacts on businesses that result in both winners and losers.

INVESTING TO UNDERSTAND CHANGE

"Some people don't like change, but you need to embrace change if the alternative is disaster." —Elon Musk, Founder, Tesla Motors, SpaceX, PayPal, etc.[2]

Combining the philosophies of both Buffett and Andreessen, there is an approach that corporations can leverage to embrace change. It starts by first taking a hard look at not only your industry but also your own business. If an entrepreneur looked at your business, would he or she see an opportunity where you have been complacent and technology could create an opening for innovation? And if so, what are the technological, societal, and marketplace changes that create this opening?

Uber for instance was able to take advantage of several trends occurring at once. The taxi industry as a whole had become incredibly complacent, charging ever-increasing fees for medallions while not investing in the consumer experience as a whole. Second, with a mobile phone in everyone's hand, technology made the on-demand economy a reality in the ability to connect two sides of a marketplace to meet supply and demand (i.e., drivers and people wanting a ride). Finally, the general public began to accept the concept of the peer-to-peer sharing economy. All combined, this opened the door for Uber (and subsequently Lyft,

Didi Kuaidi, Grab Taxi, etc.) to reinvent urban mobility. The result is the market for ride-sharing is far larger than the taxi-market ever was. In January 2016, the largest taxi company in San Francisco, Yellow Cab Cooperative, filed for bankruptcy while Uber reached a private market valuation of over $60 billion and General Motors invested $500 million for a less than 10 percent stake in Lyft.

While some companies might turn toward innovation-driven acquisition to embrace change such as this, another path is the one General Motors took with Lyft by making an investment in the startup. There are many examples of corporations successfully taking this path. Over the past five years, the number of corporate venture units worldwide has more than doubled to over 1,100; 25 of the 30 companies that comprise the Dow Jones Industrial Average have a corporate venture unit. Globally, corporate VC investors participated in $28.4 billion worth of funding across 1,301 deals in 2015, according to data from CB Insights. To put that into perspective, a corporate VC investor participated in one out of five venture-backed financing rounds, up from 16.5 percent in 2014.

Intel Capital is at the top of this list. Its corporate venture capital unit, which survived the dot-com bubble that claimed many of its peers, saw more exits since 2009 than any other VC – topping traditional venture firms such as Accel Partners and Sequoia Capital. While it does not have a formal Corporate Venture Capital unit, the advertising holding company Interpublic Group made a nearly 100X return and a profit of over $225 million in the IPO of Facebook from its 2006 investment of $2.5 million (plus a commitment to purchase $10 million in ads on the network on behalf of clients). Additionally, consider Qualcomm Ventures, which had a pretty good run in late 2015 and early 2016 with its startup investments. The company made over $100MM when the fitness tracker FitBit had its IPO in the summer of 2015. More success followed when Cruise was bought for $1 billion plus and Qualcomm was the third largest shareholder after investing only three months earlier in November 2015. All of these examples clearly deliver on Buffett's definition of investing to get more money back in the future.

MATRIX OF CORPORATE INVESTMENT

This rise in Corporate Investments comes for a multitude of reasons. *Harvard Business Review* (HBR) studied those rationales and crafted a matrix framework to map corporate VC investments. Broadly speaking, this Corporate Investment matrix is defined by two characteristics – the objective and the degree to which the operations of the investing company and the startup are linked.[3]

- **Objective**   Deals can have both financial and strategic intent. Strategic deals are made primarily to increase the sales and profits of the corporation's own businesses. Financial deals are made where a company is mainly looking for attractive returns.

- **Link to Operational Capability**   This can range from tight to loose and relates to how closely an investment relates to the current business of the corporation.

As shown in the graphic below, these two dimensions yield four types of corporate investments: Driving, Enabling, Emergent, and Passive. There is no right or wrong quadrant for a corporate investment, as each depends on the overall company strategy. It is important to note that even when the objective is more strategic by nature, capital gain must still be a driver. This aligns the incentives of the corporation, with those of the entrepreneurs they are backing and their fellow venture investors.

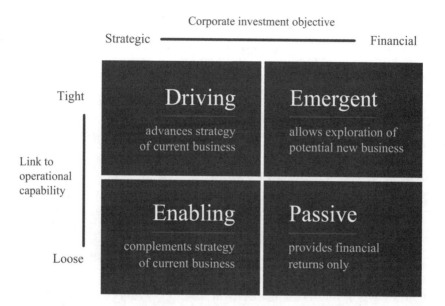

Corporate investment objective

Strategic ——————————————— Financial

	Strategic	Financial
Tight	**Driving** — advances strategy of current business	**Emergent** — allows exploration of potential new business
Loose	**Enabling** — complements strategy of current business	**Passive** — provides financial returns only

Link to operational capability

The Harvard Business Review Corporate VC Investment Matrix

With that said, a strategic objective can have multiple outcomes for both the investor and the investee. Corporate investment may be used to identify new products, services or technologies to replace existing corporate offerings. These investments can help a company gain a window into new technologies and new markets, import or enhance innovation within existing business units, or even identify potential acquisition opportunities. Another role that corporate investments may play is to complement corporate businesses by funding ventures that increase the value of the corporate ecosystem. This is a strategy that the corporate chat service Slack deployed with its recent $80 million fund, which will invest between $100,000 and $250,000 in smaller startups building applications that work with Slack's messaging service.

APPETITE FOR INVESTMENT

One traditional industry that is just starting to turn to startup investment in the face of industry change is the Packaged Food business. The food industry has faced many challenges over the last few decades from rising commodity prices to changes in government subsidies and regulations. However, two massive trends in particular are causing these businesses to re-examine their fundamental approach:

- **Rise of natural and organic**   Consumer demand has grown by double digits every year since the 1990s – and organic sales have increased from $3.6 billion in 1997 to over $39 billion in 2014. Organic food is $35.9 billion of that $39 billion. Organic and natural-food sales now represent almost 8 percent of total U.S. food sales.

- **Shift from grocery stores to restaurants**   Before the 1900s, most Americans spent 10 times more on grocery purchases than restaurant spending. By the 1950s, grocery stores made up 75 percent of the "share of food dollar." But in 2015, restaurants have grown to over 50 percent of that spending – the first time ever that Americans spent more on food from restaurants than from grocery stores.

This has led to an overall positive trend toward promoting and implementing healthier lifestyles, while medical research has focused more on related issues such as child obesity, allergies, cancer, and diabetes. As a result, the last decade has seen the rise of a new food startup industry in terms of new products, drinks, and types of food to cater to specific tastes and needs (e.g., gluten-free products). The impact has been dramatic on big brands. Between 2008 and 2013, large established brands lost 19 percent of the yogurt market and 7 percent of the coffee market to emerging brands.

With this as the backdrop, the leading food companies had several options to pursue innovation in light of the changes their industry was facing. On one hand, they could focus on the left hand side of the HBR Investment Matrix by investing in innovation and threats related to their core business of packaged food sold in retail. This could involve both "Enabling" to complement the strategy of current business (e.g., new products in current categories) or "Driving" to advance strategy of current business (i.e., new products to address needs like gluten free). Or, they could focus on "Emergent," exploring potential new businesses around *Food Tech* – examples are meal or meal-kit delivery companies – where they do not currently play. The former was the decision Tyson Foods made when they bought 5 percent of Beyond Meats, a maker of "meats" from plant proteins, in October 2016. Meanwhile, the latter would allow them to capture new growth, such as the eight million meals a month that Blue Apron ships as meal delivery kits.

The latest efforts by the major food companies appear to be focused on investing around the core, with companies such as General Mills, Coca-Cola and Campbell Soup Company all pursuing new efforts to take stakes in emerging brands. Each of these efforts come with a unique approach to investing, but the common theme appears to be consumer product companies awakening to the corporate venture opportunity.

COCA-COLA VENTURING AND EMERGING BRANDS

Sales of carbonated soft drinks have been declining for over a decade. In response, Coca-Cola launched its Venturing and Emerging Brands (VEB) group. VEB is a dedicated operating unit charged with identifying high-potential-growth brands in the beverage space for investment or ownership by The Coca-Cola Company. Put more simply, VEB's mandate is "to identify and build, and incubate the next billion-dollar brands for Coca-Cola North America."

For instance, the unit invested in ZICO Pure Premium Coconut Water in 2009 and in 2012, the company purchased a majority stake in the brand before ultimately acquiring it completely in late 2013. The same strategy was used with Honest Tea and more recently Suja Juice, the cold-pressed juice maker, where Coca-Cola paid roughly $90 million for a nearly 30 percent stake (with an option to buy them after three years). VEB also teams up with other entrepreneurial-facing firms as a way to cast a wider net over the emerging brands in the beverage industry. In partnership with the investment group and beverage incubator, L.A. Libations, Coca-Cola owns a minority stake in brands such as Aloe Gloe and Chia Via, while a partnership with the venture capital arm of First Beverage Group gives them a stake in companies like HealthAde and Essentia.

GENERAL MILLS 301 INC.

General Mills has had a venture capital firm for the past decade but announced a new initiative in 2015 called 301 INC to serve as its business development and venture capital arm. The group has made five investments including leading a $3 million round for Rhythm Superfoods, which makes snack chips from vegetables like kale and broccoli, and an investment in Beyond Meat, a maker of plant-based burgers, meatballs, and chicken strips. The group also formed a strategic partnership with CircleUp, which connects consumer and retail brand entrepreneurs to accredited investors through its online platform. 301 INC is investing earlier than you would typically expect from a major company. Tio Gazpacho is a recent investment that had sales of less than $1 million in 2015 and only has a team of two people selling its product in the New York Metro Area. General Mills recognizes that they need to provide more than just money to these startups. In particular, 301 is also offering these startups their expertise in distribution, brand building, and operations.

CAMPBELL SOUP COMPANY & ACRE VENTURE PARTNERS

"We believe that defining the future of real food requires new approaches, new business models, smart external development and an ecosystem of innovative partners." —Denise Morrison, CEO, Campbell Soup Company

Taking a different approach, the Campbell Soup Company launched an external venture fund in February 2016 called Acre Venture Partners. Campbell Soup Company is the only investor in the $125 million fund but it chose to set it up independent of the packaged food company, with only the head of its "fresh division" serving as the company's representative on Acre's investment committee. Prior to this announcement, Campbell's strategy had been acquisition versus investment. It paid $1.6 billion for the juice company Bolthouse Farms in 2012, $249 million in 2013 for baby food maker Plum Organics, and $231 million for salsa maker Garden Fresh Gourmet in 2015. The first investment by Acre was in Juicero, a food tech startup that makes internet-connected kitchen appliances. Juicero's flagship product is a $699 countertop device that cold presses juice out of "packs" of already prepped fruit and veggies (and competes with Coca-Cola VEB's investment in Suja Juice).

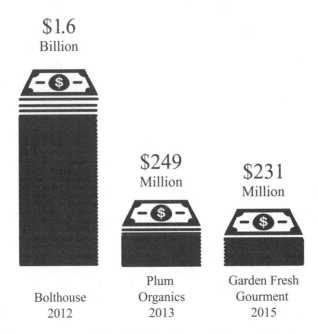

$1.6
Billion

$249
Million

$231
Million

Bolthouse
2012

Plum
Organics
2013

Garden Fresh
Gourmet
2015

The top acquisitions of Campbell Soup Company before switching from an acquisition model to an investment model in early 2016.

Outside of Acre, Campbell Soup is also investing directly in startups. In October 2016, they announced they were the sole investor in Habit, a new nutrition-focused startup that uses data from an at-home test kit to make personalized food recommendations tailored to an individual's unique DNA. While the startup's premise of combining food, well-being, and technology is interesting itself, the more intriguing part is the history between Campbell's and Habit's Founder, Neil Grimmer. Grimmer previously started Plum Organic, which grew to become the second-largest baby food brand in the U.S. before it was purchased by Campbell in 2013. Blue Chips historically have a difficult time retaining talent after an acquisition. By backing Grimmer's next entrepreneurial venture, Campbell is essentially using investment capital as outsourced R&D, backing a founder that they already believe in to build another disruptive company.

EMERGENT CORPORATE INVESTMENTS

While the major packaged food and beverage companies have mostly invested close to their core businesses, other big companies are using investment to place bets and anticipate what might happen to their businesses as technology continues to evolve. However, more importantly, they are using investing to broaden their definition of what is possible within their industries – even investing in businesses that at first blush could be competitive with their core businesses.

Consider Caterpillar, a company with over 110,000 employees, $55.2 billion in sales and 177 independently owned Cat dealerships that have their own 161,700 employees. Caterpillar invests more than $2 billion each year in research and development and holds more than 15,000 patents worldwide. Caterpillar launched Caterpillar Ventures to increase its efforts to capitalize on innovation to support customers. In May 2015, it invested in Yard Club, a San Francisco–based startup

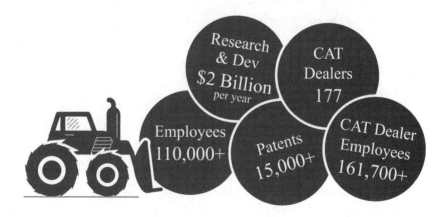

Caterpillar entered into the VC world to stay on top of innovation that could benefit Caterpillar customers.

that has developed an online peer-to-peer equipment rental platform that lets contractors rent idle equipment to each other. As part of the investment, Caterpillar also helped Yard Club launch the online ordering platform in new metropolitan markets in conjunction with U.S. and Canadian Caterpillar dealers. When announcing the deal, Caterpillar explained, "The Cat dealer will use this tool as another avenue to strengthen customer relationships by increasing the utilization rates of heavy equipment and lowering the total cost of equipment ownership." While Caterpillar invested and helped to scale Yard Club, it also avoided putting "handcuffs" on Yard Club's growth and encouraged the rental platform to include both Cat products and non-Cat branded products. This did not come without risk and convincing on the Caterpillar side. After all, the very business model of Yard Club in theory would mean that fewer customers would need to buy machines if they could rent them from their partners. However, Caterpillar Ventures General Manager Michael Young realized that the company could either

> ## "If we don't do it, someone else will."

invest in the change or lose out because of it. With the sharing economy changing the way entire industries operate, Young summed up the investment when he said, "If we don't do it, someone else will."

As the world's largest package delivery company, UPS is another Fortune 50 investing in potential new businesses that could be seen as competitive, if viewed in the wrong light. In February 2016, the UPS Strategic Enterprise Fund led a $28 million funding round in Deliv, the leading crowdsourced, same-day delivery company. Deliv was founded in 2012 to help local retailers, businesses, and e-commerce companies deliver products to customers on the same day orders come in. The company operates in 100 U.S. cities on behalf of 4,000 partners, including major retailers Macy's and Best Buy. The investment comes as the rise of same-day delivery has brought partners like Amazon and UPS into competition with each other. UPS handles about 30 percent of Amazon's 600 million packages within the United States, which is estimated to be $1 billion a year in shipping. Yet in the last few years, Amazon has added Amazon-branded trucks and negotiated to lease 20 Boeing 767 jets. With Amazon Prime Now offering same day delivery in 27 U.S. cities, Amazon has been hiring on-demand drivers through Amazon Flex. The investment in Deliv is a response to that competition and a chance for UPS to learn more about a potential new business/market, as UPS explained when discussing its investment in Deliv:

> *"Today, for UPS, we don't see the economics for same-day delivery for retail packages as currently fulfilled by Deliv. What we're doing is seeking to better understand the marketplace so it will guide our decision-making. We see this as a growing segment of the industry, so one of the reasons we invested was to learn more about the market and customer requirements and see our investments as a way to gather information to make future decisions about our business. Our Strategic Enterprise Fund continues to invest in companies that have innovative business models, and we look forward to gaining further insights into the market dynamics of same-day delivery."*

In other words, UPS is viewing this as both a strategic and potential financial investment. While the two companies technically compete in the delivery of packages, UPS views same-day delivery as an adjacent market it needs to learn more about. Rather than building its own offering, UPS is using investment as its learning tool. One day, if the organization becomes convinced of the economics of the space, this might even lead to them buying the remaining equity in Deliv. The behavior by

UPS is a strong contrast to that of rival FedEx, which in a March 2016 earnings call made the comment, "While recent stories and reports of a new entity competing with the three major carriers in the United States grabs headlines, the reality is it would be a daunting task requiring tens of billions of dollars in capital and years to build sufficient scale and density to replicate existing networks like FedEx." FedEx runs the risk of making the same mistake that Palm and Microsoft did around mobile phones, believing that insider knowledge gives it a superior competitive advantage when in reality it causes FedEx to underestimate an emerging category disruptor.

KEY TAKEAWAYS

- Corporate Venture Capital is no longer a practice just for technology companies; overall investment has risen dramatically over the last few years as incumbent companies across all industries look outside their four walls for innovation.

- The Corporate Investing matrix is defined by two characteristics: the objective and the degree to which the operations of the investing company and the startup are linked. Deals can have both financial and strategic intent. Strategic deals are made primarily to increase the sales and profits of the corporation's own businesses. Financial deals are made where a company is mainly looking for attractive returns.

- While many corporate investments complement an existing business, an increasing focus is on Emergent investments that provide corporations with a lens into potential new business models in and around their industries.

CHAPTER 5

PARTNERS FOR INNOVATION

"This is not about being best friends. It takes maturity, and is painful at times for both parties."

—Charles Redfield, Executive Vice President, Walmart, speaking about Joint Business Planning

ANY MARKETER who has worked in Consumer Packaged Goods (CPG) has at one time or another boarded a plane destined for Bentonville, Arkansas – otherwise known as the birthplace of Walmart. You make the journey to visit what is called the Home Office. Chances are you are making that trip to Home Office to participate in the annual Joint Business Plans with Walmart. Joint Business Plans (or more commonly known as JBPs) are a concept used in many industries but really gained a foothold in the lexicon of business leaders everywhere because of Walmart. The basic premise of Joint Business Planning brings the senior-most leaders from supplier companies and their peers from Walmart to the table for shared planning. As described on the Walmart Supplier Portal, 8TH & Walton:

> *"At its simplest, a joint business plan is a collaboration*
> *between retailers and suppliers in which both share insights*
> *and information, and then they work together to create a plan*

that benefits both – and the consumer. Good communication and a sense of partnership between suppliers and buyers is always a plus, but JBP involves a deeper level of alignment and collaboration, as well as more sharing of data." [1]

During my career at P&G, I spent two years working on the Walmart team, immersed in JBPs. It was during that time that I saw exactly how the concept of shared insights could result in a collaborative plan that benefits the supplier, Walmart, and the consumer. In one case, P&G wanted to grow its beauty business at Walmart through brands like Olay, Cover Girl, and Pantene. The market researchers at Procter & Gamble uncovered an important consumer insight: the Walmart shopper allocated a certain amount of time for the shopping trip and if she finished her list, she would not leave early but instead would browse other departments. The issue was that the beauty department was on the opposite side from the grocery so she rarely had enough time to make it there. The solution was to experiment with a store layout that moved the beauty department next to grocery, with the theory that the product appeal, margin, and price point would increase the overall basket size of that shopper's trip.

An idea as bold as moving an entire department would never have a chance if presented in the normal course of business between two companies. But, an idea like that is exactly within the spirit of collaboration that Joint Business Planning aspires to deliver. Walmart took the chance and in one of its new concept stores, the beauty department and grocery section were located side-by-side. As both companies hoped, shoppers loved it and the basket size of what those shoppers spent on each trip went up by double digits. JBPs are far from easy, but when they work right, the impact on the bottom line of both businesses can be outsized.

I tell that story because Joint Business Planning has become so foundational in the mindset of CPG marketers, that they have become a common format for just about any partnership that brands create. It was only fitting that when my next P&G assignment took me from Walmart to the new Digital Business Strategy team, one of the core parts of my work plan was establishing the first-ever Joint Business Plans with the four most important digital partners for P&G. In 2009, the partners were a mixture of "traditional" digital media partners (think banner and pre-roll video ads) and emerging digital marketing (search and social). On the traditional side, Yahoo and Microsoft were selected, while the emerging side included Google and Facebook. This meant that instead of boarding a plane to Bentonville, these JBPs would take us to the West Coast.

One of the very first meetings was held in Facebook's original office on University Avenue in Palo Alto, California. In January 2009, Facebook had announced it had 150 million users, passing MySpace as the largest social network in the world. By the end of 2009, Facebook had more than doubled its users to 350 million worldwide.

Because the company was going through tremendous growth, brands were trying to figure out what to do with the platform. Joint Business Planning was an unfamiliar topic in the halls of Silicon Valley; however, the timing was right for a spirit of partnership and collaboration to bring together the world's largest advertiser and the world's largest social network.

Fast forward two years later, P&G specifically talked about the relationship with Facebook when *AdAge* named the company to its Digital A-List in 2011. At the time, *AdAge* called out that "Last year [2010] P&G invested heavily in Facebook marketing to plant relationship programs inside the internet's biggest walled garden. . . . While for P&G and many marketers, 2010 was the year of acquiring Facebook fans, 2011 and beyond are for figuring out what to do with them." The JBPs started in 2009 were central to Procter & Gamble landing on the *AdAge*'s Digital A-List. The collaboration is what allowed the companies to jointly answer *AdAge*'s challenge "figuring out what to do with them."

PUTTING AN END TO STARTUP TOURISM

If you mention "partnership" with a big company to most startup founders and their venture capitalists, you will be met with eye rolls. Unfortunately, the behavior of the marketing industry as a whole has not given a lot of faith to these big business innovators that we will deliver on what we promise. Yes, there are positive examples like P&G's JBP with Facebook, but there are more bad examples. Too often, brand marketers have practiced what I call "Startup Tourism."

Startup tourism is when a big company makes a pilgrimage to where they think innovation is taking place. This might be a trip to Silicon Valley to meet with startups or taking a big group to the Consumer Electronics Show or the South by Southwest conference. When you ask the participants of the trip why they are going, they talk about "immersion" and experiencing innovation first-hand. I was guilty of this myself back at P&G when I organized a handful of these Silicon Valley immersion trips. But in my defense, at the time we did have a rhyme and reason for the trips. The majority of senior marketer leaders are not digital natives and there was a need to build muscle memory and capability around digital marketing. You could not just tell people that they should sign up for Facebook or Twitter, much less tell them they should try "check-ins" with Foursquare or set up their own blog. Their company phone was a Blackberry, not an iPhone after all. The original inspiration of these trips was to get marketers out of the office and give them a chance to see where the digital puck was heading.

Unfortunately – as we so often do as brand marketers – we have taken a good concept too far, particularly as the world has changed over the past few years. Today there should no longer be a need as marketers or business leaders to take an adult field trip for learning about digital marketing. Digital is ingrained into the very fabric of our lives and we should be forcing ourselves to experiment with new platforms every day. After all, how can you determine your brand's strategy for a new platform like Snapchat or Kik if you have not personally tried it as a consumer? Startup immersions fell down because it was a one-way street where the startups were helping a brand build its digital marketing capability but the immediate return for their help was rarely apparent outside of potential media pilots. The focus of these trips should have been on actions and results with startups, but instead success was measured by just taking part in the meeting.

STARTUPS ARE LIKE WATER

If Startup Tourism needs to end, what is the right way for brands to become engaged in the startup ecosystem and become good partners? Some of the best advice I heard on how brands should approach startups comes from Phin Barnes, who is a venture capitalist at First Round Capital. First Round is arguably the top seed-stage investor in the world. Since its inception in 2005, the VC firm has backed over 300 companies, including being the first investor in companies such as Uber, Square, Warby Parker, and many more. I've known Phin since his days building a videogame called Yourself!Fitness, the first fitness game for Xbox and PlayStation 2. In fact, we met through working together to craft a promotional partnership between Yourself!Fitness and Secret Deodorant, the brand I was working on at the time. Phin has seen all kinds of partnerships between brands and startups, both from the seat of an investor but also as a founder himself. He gives very valuable advice to brands:

> *"Startups are like water. They will take the easiest path down the hill."*

The point Phin is making is that startups do not necessarily care that you are from a big company or that you control one of the largest marketing budgets in the industry. In fact, that might be a liability for them in regards to working with you. Startups want to find a brand that will be a good partner – someone who will respect their time, make quick decisions, and not take a dozen meetings in order to get something finalized. That is the issue with traditional Startup immersion trips – they are filled with a false promise.

There is nothing more valuable than time for a startup; each of them is working against a clock that is called their burn rate. The majority of the startups have raised a certain amount of venture capital and each month, their bank account goes down a certain amount (this is burn rate). Yes, they have revenue coming in but it is rare – especially for an early stage company – that their inflows cover their outflows each month. Thus, when a big company reaches out for a meeting, a startup needs to see the potential in the meeting to move its business forward. Startups do not have the luxury of

There is nothing more valuable than time for a startup.

time or waiting for the next fiscal year for a test and learn. They need to find the quickest and easiest path down the hill.

On the other side of the table, big companies have their own criteria in the early days of exploring a partnership. At the 2016 South by Southwest conference, Jaime Fabricant of PepsiCo Beverages spoke on a panel called "Naked Partnerships: Brand–Startup Partnerships in Real Life." During the panel, Jamie discussed how the food and beverage giant is using three rules to guide its choices around working with startups including:

- **Has this never been done before?** PepsiCo is one brand that wants to be on the leading edge. It believes in looking for white space, which often leads to a unique engagement opportunity. For instance, Pepsi very early on sponsored the NYC leaderboard on Foursquare, donating to a local charity for every check-in.

- **Can it scale?** While Pepsi wants to be early, it also needs to be able to take an innovative program and, following initial tests, expand its reach when desired.

- **What is the business model?** The definition of a business model is changing. One driver should be traditional product sales; however, it can go beyond that and be monetized in a multitude of ways.[2]

Big companies are immune to the struggles of time and money startups go through. Meanwhile, startups do not understand the inherent barriers to innovation that Blue Chips face. Partnership requires openness on both sides and the exploration of new models for working together.

MANY MODELS OF PARTNERSHIPS

"I think we have only begun to see what can happen when startups and big companies, especially multinationals, mash up to create new types of ventures. I'm not talking about big companies funding or mentoring startups. I mean when both startups and big companies understand what each brings to the table and actually codesign, building new things that couldn't happen any other way." —David Butler, Vice President of Innovation, Coca-Cola[3]

Many of the best marketers have opened their eyes to the need for a new way of working between brands and startups.

To get there, multiple models of experimentation have emerged. Some brands are opening up offices in Silicon Valley and other innovation hubs across the globe to bring them closer to startups. Others have turned to great outside firms like Kite, Pilot44, or BrandGarage that serve as brand innovation matchmakers. Brands have even opened up their own Startup Accelerators and Incubators in order to build partnerships. When you talk to the most respected brands that are leading this change, you realize that no one approach is universally right. Every single option has its own pros and cons that will frankly change based on the corporate culture within which it is working.

Nevertheless, there is a common thread in the most successful relationships between brands and startups. In fact, those relationships that work are not any different than those Joint Business Plans between big companies. They are built on collaboration and partnership, where working together is mutually beneficial. This takes effort from everyone involved and will take companies out of their comfort zones.

The big company cannot think it has power over the startup because of its size; in addition, big companies cannot expect to get something for nothing just so the startup can say it worked with you (in other words, no free pilots or test and learns). Likewise, the startup cannot view the big company as a naïve "piggy bank" that provides alternative funding or just another logo for its investor pitch deck. Both sides need to be open about their goals and objectives, as well as any barriers that might exist in making the partnership a success. Fortunately, there are several industry leaders who set great examples of building these successful relationships.

Banking

As one of the more regulated industries, banking does not immediately come to mind as an industry that would be leaning into relationships with emerging startups. The emergence of FinTech (short for Financial Technology) is changing that. Almost every type of financial activity – from banking to payments to wealth management and more – is being re-imagined by startups. In response, big companies have turned to both acquisition and investment.

Citi Ventures has focused on the future of commerce and payments, as well as financial technology through investments in Square, Betterment, Jumio and Docusign. They have also launched Citi FinTech, a skunk-works operation of 40 employees focused on the future of banking. Ally Financial has gone the acquisition route, purchasing online broker TradeKing for $275 million and giving it access to the company's robo-advisor platform. Robo-advisors, which manage client assets via computer algorithms for a low fee, have emerged as a real threat to tra-ditional wealth management, with growth of 200 percent in assets under management in 2015 alone. While acquisition and investment have their place, the banking industry has also shown that partnership can be a viable path to create mutually beneficial relationships:

- **Santander & Funding Circle**   In June 2014, peer-to-peer lending platform Funding Circle announced a first of its kind partnership with Santander UK, in which the bank would proactively refer small business customers looking for a loan. In return, Funding Circle would promote Santander to borrowers on their platform when they require day-to-day relationship banking. The deal involved no revenue sharing and focused on a mutually beneficial relationship where both parties focused on their respective strengths. In speaking about the deal, the Founder of Funding Circle reinforced this collaboration: "In Santander we have found a fellow challenger brand that shares our commitment to putting small business customers' needs first. They have created a blueprint for other banks to follow."

- **Citigroup & Lending Club**   In a different sort of partnership, Lending Club and Citi have collaborated to facilitate up to $150 million in loans to low-income borrowers in underserved communities under the Community Reinvestment Act (CRA). The mutual win gives Citi credit for making CRA loans without having to find and vet borrowers, while Lending Club will get new customers with certainty that there will be a funder for their loans.

Telecom

Taking a different approach, several of the largest players in the telecom industry have formed a partnership not only with startups, but also amongst themselves. Deutsche Telekom, Orange, Singtel and Telefonica launched a startup ecosystem alliance under the Go Ignite brand. The initiative is a partnership between the company innovation arms – Singtel Innov8, Orange Fab, hub:raum, and Telefonica Open Future – and will help eligible startups across Southeast Asia, Africa, Europe, Latin America, and the Middle East. Selected startups will benefit from the alliance members' collective resources, such as the opportunity to gain access to

Go Ignite alliance members' business units and their collective customer base, which includes enterprises and consumers and equates to over one billion mobile customers across five continents.

Consumer Packaged Goods

"We spend a lot of time doing planning and perfecting. What startups do is launch and learn. It's good for us." —Kevin Weed, Chief Marketing Officer, Unilever

Perhaps the most active industry in terms of partnerships with startups comes from Consumer Packaged Goods (CPG). Given that CPG brands are historically among the largest advertisers and most active marketers, this fact is not surprising. By nature, it is an industry that is externally focused on finding new ways to reach consumers. That is why some of the earliest efforts in partnerships came out of CPG programs like PepsiCo10. The biggest shift for most CPG companies is the need to reapply that Joint Business Planning mindset so they are able to build real partnerships with startups, not just execute media buys with small test-and-learn budgets.

- ■ **Procter & Gamble Brandery Fellowship**   Announced in 2015, P&G works with the Brandery (the startup accelerator that I co-founded) to identify two companies in each class for partnership. With the Brandery located in P&G's hometown of Cincinnati, Ohio, it presents an opportunity for very hands-on involvement that goes beyond a paid pilot. This program includes direct access to P&G mentors, active connections with P&G brand teams, and engagement with senior P&G executives. In order to find the highest caliber companies, P&G identifies very specific focus areas that can help its brands solve immediate business needs. The challenges identified in the first year led P&G to work with Skip, a company offering a mobile-based, in-store checkout technology, and AdAdapted, a platform that automates native advertising for mobile apps.

■ **Unilever Foundry**   Launched in 2014, The Foundry united and expanded Unilever's existing efforts to work with startups. The Foundry's purpose is to serve as the entry point for innovative tech companies seeking to connect with Unilever. Like many programs, Foundry facilitates paid pilots for startups and also creates opportunities for startups and brands to meet in networking events, Hacks, and competitions. One unique differentiator is the Foundry Mentors program, which partners startups with one of Unilever's 7,000 marketers for three months to develop their brand positioning, marketing strategy, and product roadmap. Another is Foundry 50, a partnership between Unilever and the Cannes Lions Innovation to bring 50 of the best marketing technology startups to meet the industry at Cannes.

■ **Nestlé Silicon Valley Innovation Outpost**   Over the last few years, hundreds of big companies have set up innovation outposts in Silicon Valley. Steve Blank summed up the results best when he wrote that, "the reality is that to date, most of these Innovation Outposts are at best another form of innovation theater – they make a large company feel like they're innovating, but very few of these outposts change a company's product direction and fewer impact their bottom line."[4] One of the exceptions to this rule is Nestlé. Unlike many of its peers, Nestlé didn't seek headlines around its establishment of an office in San Francisco, which has been operating since 2013. The company did not hire people from Google or Apple to run the office in the hopes they would magically bring along the innovation culture of their former employer. Instead, Nestlé turned to two of its veterans – Stephanie Naegeli and Mark Brodeur – that had deep ties to Nestlé World Headquarters in Switzerland and in Nestlé North America. With strong connections with their operating units and an executive-level champion at headquarters, this allowed the Nestlé team at the Innovation Outpost to drive real partnerships that impact the bottom line, not just generate headlines. The team has continued this leadership with the launch of HENRi (https://henri.nestle.com), an external innovation platform that was built on the best practices of startup partnership. On HENRi, Nestlé posts business challenges that start with a clearly written brief that is open for 45 days, assigned funding of $50,000, and the backing of a senior executive sponsor. As a result, Nestlé has built a program where the Blue Chip has "skin in the game" with financial support, leadership of a sponsor to make it happen, and a short time frame to move at a speed that is more in line with the needs of startups.

UNDERSTANDING THE MINDSET ON BOTH SIDES

Partnerships can be one of the more useful collaboration tools for brands and startups. Partnerships are usually the first step in many cases given the flexibility and lack of permanence that come from an investment or acquisition. With that said, good partnerships are difficult. Partnerships take time, commitment and collaboration to build relationships that work and deliver value. Brands and startups both have to put skin in the game. A partnership should not be a path to generating PR – either PR around your big company being "innovative" or about your startup working with a big client. It needs to be about a partnership that delivers real financial results that create value on both sides.

In order to create this value, it is important to understand the mindset of both sides. This is something that most Blue Chips have never had to do. Traditionally, big companies worked mostly with other big companies. Big brand worked with big retailer. Or big media company. Or big advertising agency. In all of these partnerships, the people on each side of the table are more similar than they are different. Both sides work for large companies where they generally have the security of a comfortable salary, the clarity of how to succeed in their career path, and the respect that comes with a job at a Fortune 500.

That is not the case when working with Startups, particularly early stage companies. Despite my experience as an investor and advisor to these companies and their founders, I often say "I am not an entrepreneur." While people might give me quizzical looks with that statement, I say it because an entrepreneur has gone through a life experience that is unique. Unless you have personally experienced it, there is no way for someone employed by a Blue Chip to realize what it is like to go 18 months without a real paycheck, piling on personal debt, and working toward a future that is hazy at best. Every day an entrepreneur is told no. They have to persuade customers, investors, and employees to believe in their vision for creating something great. They are on a roller coaster of wins and losses, failures and successes. In that journey, the partnership with a big company might just be a "make it or break it deal."

> **I often say "I am not an entrepreneur"; an entrepreneur has gone through a life experience that is unique.**

As such, it is critically important to have a level of empathy for startups when structuring a partnership and being a true partner. Early stage companies are volatile and fragile by their very nature. As a result, working with them will require a different mindset than other partnerships. If a Blue Chip embraces it instead of shying away, it can view things in a different perspective as it sits at the negotiating table. It might feel uncomfortable or even scary. That is the nature of innovation. It is far from easy and rarely follows the same path that has been done before. Or, as Peter Thiel wrote in *Zero to One*: "Today's 'best practices' lead to dead ends; the best paths are new and untried."

KEY TAKEAWAYS

- ■ One successful model for forming partnerships in the startup world is to reapply the Joint Business Plan format, which has worked successfully between brands and retailers.

- ■ Startup Tourism by big brands has made some startups (and their investors) reluctant to believe in the promises of partnerships. Big brands need to show an understanding and appreciation of the startup culture to overcome these reservations.

- ■ Partnerships between brands and startups require that both sides have "skin in the game" and are committed to real results.

- ■ Big companies need to understand the unique mindset of entrepreneurs and early stage Startups. Having empathy is critically important to being a true partner.

The Brandery

Consistently ranked as one of the top startup accelerators in the world, The Brandery has graduated over 65 companies from the program that have raised nearly $150 million in Venture Capital. Over six years, the accelerator has evaluated more than 5,000 early-stage startups that have applied for a spot in the annual program. Additionally, the accelerator supports a yearly event called Brand Fusion, which is essentially a "speed dating" event between brand marketers and venture-backed startups where 350 meetings take place. As a result of these efforts, The Brandery has learned a few lessons on how to evaluate what makes a startup standout from a crowded field. As co-founder of the program, I share my take on how Blue Chips can use these same lessons to evaluate potential startup partnerships:

As a startup accelerator, The Brandery is generally focused on early-stage startups that have received limited investment. This means the teams are generally two to five people, the company is under two years old, and if they have raised any money, it was likely a seed round of funding that was less than $1.5 million. Said another way, the startup is missing much of the "external validation" that you might see from a later-stage startup. There is not a brand name Venture Capital firm that led an eight-digit investment into the startup. TechCrunch – much less the *Wall Street Journal* – has not done a front-page write-up on the company. These are not "unicorns" but instead new companies at the very beginning of their entrepreneurial journey. Adding to the challenge is that "applications" take place over a condensed time period. Companies apply in February through April every year. Finalists are selected from the applicant pool, interviews take place in less than four week in late April through early May, and offers are extended to ten startups. With this timeline, deep due diligence is just not an option.

The result is the team at The Brandery has developed its own unique way of evaluating the potential of startups. Every person that sits on the selection committee has different criteria that they are looking for as they review applications and sit through interviews. That in itself is one of the first takeaways in the process. The Brandery has a diverse team, each coming from a different professional background ranging from big brand and digital marketing to legal and startup founder. That diversity of thought helps us to look at a startup from every angle and possibly see something that others might have missed. There is a natural tension in these differing opinions but that very tension is what sparks productive debate around the pro's and con's of each startup. Big Companies should follow this same practice, leveraging a diverse team approach versus counting on a single department, function, or decision maker to evaluate potential partners.

With that diversity of thought as a backstop, I have my own criteria of what I look for when a company applies for The Brandery. These include:

- **Inspiration**   One of my personal favorite types of startups come when a founder is "scratching an itch." This comes when they have uncovered something that they want to solve so bad that it keeps them up at night. They are not chasing a market but solving a problem that they want solved. Drew Houston had this sort of inspiration for Dropbox when he was on a bus to New York and could not work on the four-hour ride from Boston because he forgot the USB memory stick with the files he wanted to work on.

- **Tenacity**   The interesting thing about great founders is that they often have many other professional options that would be more financially rewarding – or at least safer financially – than working on what they are pursuing. Investors pay attention to "pedigrees" and they want founders that are alumni of great schools like Harvard and Stanford or marquee tech companies like Google and Facebook. That same pedigree means that when the going gets tough with a startup, those founders have plenty of other options to something different. As such, I want a founder with the tenacity to keep going even through the deepest and darkest valleys. The ones that double down when things are the toughest instead of looking for an easy way out. There is such a thing as "Founder Tourism," those entrepreneurs who love the concept of launching a startup but do not really have the stomach for it.

- **Team**   Just as there is value in a diverse team to evaluate startups, it is even more important that there is a diverse team building the startup. Tech startups in particular require a diverse skill set to get off the ground. Dave McClure, the famous investor/entrepreneur behind 500 startups, describes the perfect formula behind the team as a "Hacker, Hustler, and Designer." The Hacker is the developer, the person writing the code. The Hustler is the leader of the team, the one doing every job and task possible to clear the way for the team to work. Finally, the Designer is the one to bring the visual expertise, creating the great user experience and brand.

■ **Insight**   Research has shown time and time again that the "first-mover advantage" is often a fallacy. Facebook was not the first social network. Google was not the first search engine. As such, I am not worried if there is competition when a startup presents what they are doing. What I want to hear is the insight on what is missing in those competitors. What does the founder see that others do not and how will that be a wedge that allows them to win. Competition can actually be a great motivator to build something better.

■ **Aligned Goals**   The final criteria is one that applies for any relationship dynamic that exists within a startup. This includes the founders, the investors, the employees, and even eventual partners or acquirers. Long-term success starts and ends with the Aligned Goals. I want to see that the founders have had this talk and are aligned on what type of company that they want to build. With that, I hope to see that they are only looking for investors and partners that share that vision instead of just looking for a checkbook.

I have found these criteria can go beyond just early-stage startups that are applying for Accelerator. This same grading – with some slight tweaks – has also worked well when matching startups with Blue Chips. In the end, no model is perfect but instead it is about knowing what things matter most to your business and what you are looking for in a partner.

CHAPTER 6

DISRUPT THE DISRUPTORS

"Your margin is my opportunity."

—Jeff Bezos, CEO, Amazon.com

WHEN NAMING HIM the 2012 Businessperson of the Year, *Fortune Magazine* called Jeff Bezos "the ultimate disruptor: the man who has upended the book industry and displaced electronics merchants." Bezos has done so much by following his favorite aphorism around margins – acting as a living, breathing example of Clayton Christenen's classic definition of Disruptive Innovation. Christensen recapped that definition in *Harvard Business Review* recently when he wrote:

> *"Disruption describes a process whereby a smaller company with fewer resources is able to successfully challenge established incumbent businesses. Specifically, as incumbents focus on improving their products and services for their most demanding (and usually most profitable) customers, they exceed the needs of some segments and ignore the needs of others. Entrants that prove disruptive begin by successfully targeting those overlooked segments, gaining a foothold by delivering more-suitable functionality – **frequently at a lower price.***

Incumbents, chasing higher profitability in more-demanding
segments, tend not to respond vigorously. Entrants then
move upmarket, delivering the performance that incumbents'
mainstream customers require, while preserving the advantages
that drove their early success. When mainstream customers
start adopting the entrants' offerings in volume, disruption has
occurred."

The approach Bezos has taken to retail with Amazon.com followed this path perfectly; disruption has clearly occurred with mainstream customers. Nearly twenty years after the company went public, it has reached over $100 billion in sales, the fastest a company has ever reached the mark.

Yet, Amazon is not a company content with just being a disruptor around retail. Bezos reveres invention. It is what led the company to launch Amazon Web Services, a division that has reached $10 billion in sales and has done so at a faster rate than its parent company did. It led to the Amazon Kindle, which brought e-readers mainstream, and Amazon Echo, which is turning into the company's "Trojan Horse" in the battle for the connected home and of "voice" as the new operating system. Bezos talked about this love of invention in his 2015 Shareholder Letter, writing:

> *"We want to be a large company that's also an invention*
> *machine. We want to combine the extraordinary customer-*
> *serving capabilities that are enabled by size with the speed of*
> *movement, nimbleness, and risk-acceptance mentality normally*
> *associated with entrepreneurial start-ups."*

Looking at Amazon's actions, it is approaching invention in two ways. Efforts like the Echo are truly groundbreaking inventions. These inventions are what Kai-Fu Lee, the CEO of China-based Innovation Works, described as ". . . a Larry-and-Sergey phenomenon . . . people who think of things that users don't even know that they want, and who really build something that wows people. People who do the really unpopular thing that ends up changing the world." In addition, Amazon focuses on a second type of invention, one where it improves on an invention that is already in the market. The launch of the Kindle in 2007 followed a decade of e-book readers that started after the establishment of the E Ink Corporation in 1997. This occurrence is not unusual in business. After all, Facebook was not the first social network. It was built upon the lessons of MySpace, Bebo, Friendster, and countless others. Apple's iPod was actually the thirteenth MP3 player on the market.

Amazon has perfected this art of a dual strategy for invention, particularly improving upon an existing player. As Bezos described it, "You want to look at what other companies are doing. But you don't want to look at it as if, 'Okay, we're going to copy that.' You want to look at it and say, 'That's very interesting. What can we be inspired to do as a result of that?' And then put your own unique twist on it." The Kindle is an obvious example, but Amazon has taken this approach multiple

What can we be inspired to do as a result of that?

times. Its MyHabit site, which is a private sales site featuring upscale and designer fashion, borrows from flash site pioneers like Gilt Groupe and Rue La La. Amazon Local was an attempt to capitalize on the once hot daily deals space of Groupon and Living Social. Even Prime Now, Amazon's efforts in same-day delivery that launched in Manhattan in December 2014, is based on a same-day local delivery business model created by the startup Deliv two years earlier.

At Procter & Gamble, we called this practice "search and reapply" where you look for best practices and bring them into your business. The former President of PepsiCo wrote in the *Harvard Business Review* that they also practiced this behavior when he said that, "most of PepsiCo's major strategic successes are ideas we borrowed from the marketplace – often from small regional or local competitors." In today's world of constant innovation, I think the more appropriate description for this practice of borrowing inspiration would be "Disrupt the Disruptors." When Bezos speaks about the advantages of size combined with the speed of entrepreneurial startups, he's referring to this very strategy.

Consider the aforementioned Amazon Prime Now, which launched only 111 days after the project got the green light. In the summer of 2014, Deliv announced partnerships with 30 mall properties and expansion of its service to five new cities. Moving to not only counter this competitive threat but also seize the market opportunity Deliv had shown, it took Amazon less than four months to "build a customer-facing app, secure a location for an urban warehouse, determine which 25,000 items to sell, get those items stocked, recruit new staff, test, iterate, design new software for internal use – both a warehouse management system and a driver-facing app – and launch in time for the holidays."

Amazon used its scale and resources, combined with its entrepreneurial spirit to move at the speed of a startup to capitalize on an opportunity. Fast forward to today and Amazon's competitors like Macy's and Best Buy are turning to Deliv to fulfill the last mile of local, same-day delivery – giving up control of that consumer touchpoint. Meanwhile Amazon has expanded Prime Now into 30 cities, giving Amazon its own proprietary way to own the consumer relationship, in a way their traditional competitors can only dream of.

BEAT THEM AT THEIR OWN GAME

"Everybody talks about disruption until you actually f—ing disrupt something and then everybody freaks the f— out." —Shane Smith, founder of Vice Media

As big companies address the threat and opportunity of the innovation economy, the strategies of invest, acquire, or partner are all potential responses. In addition, a fourth strategy is to disrupt the disruptor and beat the innovators at their own game. Unlike traditional competitors, startups do not attack existing players head-on. Instead, startups go around incumbents, and it takes a while before bigger companies feel their market presence. However, with strong market intelligence, big companies can see the innovators coming. They can use the innovators as inspiration and then leverage their own scale to turn the tables by actually attacking the startup directly.

The concept is not about acquiring a startup like Amazon did with Zappos or Diapers.com. Instead, it is about identifying innovations early and then using the scale of the big company to execute them. While this strategy is not focused on acquisition, the same three categories can be used to classify the behaviors.

Core

The safest approach for disrupting the disruptor is what might be called "one-degree innovation." In this method, you take inspiration from the efforts of an innovative startup and apply it to your core business. This implementation does not come with a dramatic departure from your business but instead aims to complement the current strategy.

The hotel chain Hyatt uses this approach as it looks to embrace changing consumer preferences – whether that is Airbnb or the rise of a "craft culture" that is seeking brands with a story behind them. In March 2016 it launched the Unbound Collection by Hyatt, a global collection of unique and independent stay experiences at properties such as The Driskill Hotel in Austin, Texas or the Hôtel du Louvre in Paris, France. This effort partners with properties that have a rich social currency and are "story-worthy" with travel experiences outside of the hotel itself.

The efforts are not a dramatic departure from the core business of Hyatt, but an Enabling strategy that takes a step toward the future. Also, before launching the Unbound Collection, Hyatt used investing to develop its market intelligence around lodging innovators like Airbnb and Homeaway. It did this by investing in OneFineStay, a London-based startup for private rentals of high-end luxury homes combined with a hotel-like service for hosts and travelers. Hyatt's competitor Accor Hotels took that market intelligence a step further by acquiring OneFineStay in April 2016 for around $170 million, committing to invest another $70+ million so it can remain operating as an independent company.

Adjacent

The second approach for disrupting the disruptor is with adjacent innovation, which means entering a new neighboring market to the one the business currently serves. The innovation is often "new to the company," but not in a category or market because it is a dramatic departure from its core business. One example that has been common in traditional innovation occurs when a company that sells physical products moves into the service industry, but in the same category where it has history. Valvoline Motor Oil launching Valvoline Instant Oil Change to move in the quick lube service industry is one such instance.

A recent example of this adjacent innovation by Blue Chips can be found in the on-demand laundry and dry cleaning space. Aiming to be the Uber for laundry, nearly 50 startups such as Washio, Cleanly, and Rinse are taking aim at the estimated $10 billion industry. They are doing so by providing a mobile app that lets users schedule laundry pickup and delivery from their phones. Washio is the largest with projected sales of $20 million but has only launched in six cities. Recognizing an opportunity to bring its scale to the category, Tide Detergent – which is owned by Procter & Gamble – launched Tide Spin in Chicago.

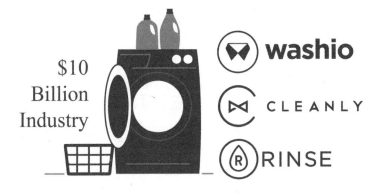

Aiming to be the Uber for laundry, nearly 50 startups such as Washio, Cleanly, and Rinse are taking aim at the estimated $10 billion industry.

Out-of-home laundry services are not a threat to the core business of Tide, which has over 30 percent market share of the $7.2 billion laundry detergent category. After all, Tide has co-existed with the dry cleaning industry for its entire existence and P&G has even launched franchises of Tide Dry Cleaners to compete in that segment. Entering the on-demand laundry space gives Tide the opportunity to move into an adjacent category that could drive not only incremental sales, but possibly incredible margin, as well. Existing innovators like Washio have proven the consumer interest in the model and now P&G can launch a disruptor that leverages the resources of Tide to drive adoption of its own offering.

Emergent

The final approach to disrupting the disruptors comes from emergent innovation that can take a big company into a new business model. The result might be an entirely new business unit for the parent company or even a fundamental change in the company as a whole. The latter approach happens most often when a company realizes that a new innovation could lead to its extinction. Think about what digital cameras have done to Kodak.

The defining example of a company employing this approach is Netflix – the company that brought binge watching to households worldwide. It was less than 10 years ago that Netflix was almost entirely a DVD-by-mail business. However, in the late 2000s, Hulu introduced video streaming, Amazon debuted Instant Video, and Apple launched iTunes. Netflix CEO Reed Hastings realized that the future of Netflix was not going to be physically mailing DVDs, but instead embraced the technology trends that were enabling streaming video to become the default mode for video rentals. Faced with this potential disruption, Hastings used the resources, brand, and cash flow of Netflix's core business to invest in streaming. As Hastings told investors in 2011, "Our future is brightest by focusing on streaming." In less than a year, Netflix shifted from the fastest-growing customer of the United States Postal Service first-class mail service to the biggest source of evening internet traffic in North America. Today, the company has over 75 million subscribers and accounts for over 30 percent of internet traffic. With this strategy, Netflix not only disrupted the disruptors, but it also disrupted itself.

A RIGHT TO INNOVATE

"We must have a healthy disrespect for our current business model."

—J.B. Kropp, VP of Digital Strategy and Business Development, E.W. Scripps Company

This is far from easy. In fact, many big companies are not naturally wired to disrupt the disruptors. As publicly traded companies that have to answer to Wall Street each quarter, they are more focused on driving marginal profitability from their existing business versus launching innovative projects that might cannibalize those existing businesses. As a result, they do not recognize the emerging threat from a startup until it is impacting the bottom line of their current business. Consider the example of Dollar Shave Club. When the service launched in 2012, a spokesperson for Gillette told the *Wall Street Journal* that, "the shaving giant isn't worried about losing market share, in part because other subscription-based companies have tried and failed." But two years later, as Dollar Shave was eating away market share, Gillette launched a subscription service with its CFO stating in an earnings call, "With more men purchasing their blades and razors through e-commerce, it's critical that Gillette establishes itself as the online leader." Contrast that with the viewpoint of E.W. Scripps where they realized that high stakes business requires a healthy disrespect of the current way of doing things before it is too late.

As the strategies in the previous section show, there are ways for big companies to fight back with their own efforts in the face of innovation. Doing so requires taking a look both at your own company, as well as the external market, to consider a few key strategic questions:

1. **What parts of the disruptor's business model make them unique?**
Most startups have several unique aspects that only work as a sum of
the parts. The monthly subscription aspect of Dollar Shave Club was
new for the shaving category, but it was only one part of the appeal.
Dollar Shave Club combined it with a price point significantly lower
than the market average, along with a go-to-market strategy that
was more Direct Marketing (i.e. cost per acquisition) than Brand
Marketing (cost per impression). A big company cannot stand up
a single part of the business model without looking at the business
model in totality. You cannot cherry pick the part of the business
that is easiest to replicate.

2. **What barriers to entry exist in "copying" the efforts of the
disruptor?** By their very nature, disruptors tend to focus on
underserved parts of the market. They are not able to "throw
money" at a problem and thus, they take different and creative
approaches than the incumbents. This often results in building
a more competitive advantage that is unfamiliar territory for
the incumbents. For instance, many of today's startups have a
marketplace element to them and several are even two-sided
marketplaces. Uber is a two-sided marketplace with people willing
to be drivers and those looking for a ride. Airbnb is the same with
those willing to rent out their homes and those seeking a place to
stay. While many big companies have plenty of experience in using
marketing to drive demand and consumption, they are more used to
"buying" supply rather than creating it. Hilton knows how to build
or buy a hotel to increase its inventory of rooms, but it doesn't have
experience convincing homeowners that it would be better to list
their houses on a Hilton peer-to-peer site like Airbnb does.

3. **Does the disruptor have an inherent cost advantage that would be difficult to replicate?** As startups focus on attacking a market, they will often look to exploit pricing inefficiencies in order to gain an upper hand. One such approach is changing the value chain, often eliminating "middlemen" that exist between the brand and the consumer. This in turn creates a cost advantage that often becomes difficult for a big company to replicate. For example, in the mattress category, Casper goes direct to consumers instead of mattress stores that would mark up the cost. Casper is then able to reinvest that margin into shipping the mattress directly to consumers and at a lower price.

4. **What competitive advantages would a big company bring to the market?** People may expect that startups seek out partnerships with larger companies for financial resources. However, this is not always the case; often times the big company can bring a competitive advantage that will help accelerate growth for the startup. That same reasoning can create an advantage for a big company to move into a market. For instance, the Tide brand brings instant credibility that the clothes will come back clean to the on-demand laundry space. No one doubted the ability of Amazon to have a deep inventory of books available for the Kindle given its strong relationships with book publishers (unlike Sony, who launched one of the first e-readers).

For some companies, examining these areas will lead to the realization that launching your own efforts might not be the best approach. And, that's okay. Investment, acquisition, and partnership are all sound, time-tested strategies. Yet, there is an equal chance that answering these questions will lead to an opportunity to use the brand, cash flow or resources of the big company to move into an area of disruptive innovation.

"The best way to predict the future is to continue to invent it."

—David Glass, former President and Chief Executive Officer, Walmart Stores, Inc.

KEY TAKEAWAYS

- ▣ Incumbents have an opportunity to "disrupt the disruptors," taking inspiration from a startup or innovative competitor and using their scale, brand, and financial resources to launch a new effort.

- ▣ The strategy of "disrupt the disruptor" has the same three categories as acquisition in Core, Adjacent, and Emergent. Acquiring and scaling an innovator early on is an alternative strategy to launching a competitive effort.

- ▣ Not all big companies are currently built for this approach; thus, they need to take an honest look at both internal and external conditions to determine if they have the right structure.

THE TURN

Nestlé

Pete Blackshaw is the Vice President of Digital and Social Media at Nestlé, S.A. based in Switzerland. In addition to helping shape digital strategy for Nescafe, Kit Kat, Purina, and hundreds of other Nestlé brands, Pete oversees Nestlé's industry-recognized Digital Acceleration Team (DAT) as well as the Silicon Valley Innovation Outpost (SVIO). He is author of Satisfied Customers Tell Three Friends, Angry Customers Tell 3,000: Running a Business in Today's Consumer-Driven World (Doubleday), and periodically authors columns in Advertising Age centered around the book's themes. Pete founded PlanetFeedback.com, one of the web's first consumer-feedback portals, and co-founded the Word-of-Mouth Marketing Association (WOMMA).
Pete Blackshaw:

"Can a 150-year-old company act like a startup?" This is the question I've asked myself every day since I joined Nestlé.

It's fair to be skeptical. After all, Nestlé is the world's largest food and beverage company. It has 340,000 employees across more than 100 markets and 2,000 brands. Most companies of such size and scale can be unbearably slow and impenetrably bureaucratic. They have no shortage of processes and compliance obligations to manage. Supply chain imperatives alone demand thoughtful and methodical deliberation, and with little margin for error.

Moreover, the marketplace can be unforgiving when large companies make mistakes, especially with social media keeping tabs on everything. Indeed, "tall trees get the wind," we often say in the context of issues management. Still, our industry is undergoing dramatic if not disruptive change. We're feeling it most profoundly in the marketing and sales context, but digital disruption touches every aspect of the enterprise.

As Davos 2016 literature noted so well in the context of what they dubbed the 4th Industrial revolution, "We stand on the brink of a technological revolution that will fundamentally alter the way we live, work, and relate to one another. In its scale, scope, and complexity, the transformation will be unlike anything humankind has experienced before."

Against this backdrop, everything must change. Nothing can be taken for granted. And the corporate enterprise has no choice but to double down in driving – if not leading – transformation.

And so, "Can a 150-year-old company act like a startup?" I believe it can, and I'd like to share a few examples of how we've been making progress.

But first, some background. I joined Nestlé in 2011, and this is my second "tour," so to speak, leading digital in a large company. My first foray was at P&G in the late 1990s. In between I founded a venture-funded startup that eventually was sold to Nielsen and wrote a book about customer service and social media.

Why did I return to a large company? Candidly, I relish being a change agent. I also sensed genuine desire by Nestlé to not merely play catch-up, but to lead. And even disrupt. And this is always attractive to entrepreneurs. It was also clear in coming to Nestlé that the opportunity I faced far transcended the brand management and marketing world scope of my P&G work and experience.

Today the digital leader is not merely tweaking the marketing mix, or figuring out the next variant of the banner ad, but more importantly, inspiring a new model for the enterprise.

INNOVATION, CULTURE AND SPEED

Throughout my career I've maintained that digital is as much an operating principle as a communication channel. And the operating principles are what have the greatest potential to transform the enterprise. Here are three ways we've driven innovation at Nestlé: internal innovation, externally focused innovation, and open innovation.

INTERNAL INNOVATION

I'm a big believer in the concept of "constructive paranoia." How can we make a large enterprise restless, impatient, and even a little insecure about how well it's pacing with the new reality – and in such a way that it motivates tangible, concrete, and often fast action?

And so one of my first actions after I arrived at Nestlé was bringing top executives to the Silicon Valley. There we invested time early on studying the "hackathon" and "lean start-up" culture so visible at Facebook, Google, and many small startups that were creating value at astonishing speeds.

We were taken – even humbled – by the fast, highly-iterative problem solving. This helped precipitate a creation program we call the DAT, or Digital Acceleration Team.

The word "Acceleration" says it all. We sought a new approach to speed, agility and brand building – and later, e-commerce – and with an eye toward fast-deployment to the markets.

Anchored by the three pillars – Listening, Engaging, and Transforming – the program is made up of 18 high-potential managers – virtually all Millennials – who rotate in our headquarters every eight months. They work in an entrepreneurial workspace that includes live listening screens and a multi-media content studio for sharing best practices. We deliberately nested it above our executive suite.

Is this having an impact? We've already graduated over 110 high-potential managers across seven classes and 50 participating markets, from China and Vietnam to Ecuador to Trinidad and Tobago. They will return to our markets to power digital and e-commerce as well as business transformation. And they are assuming core roles in brand, media, sales and beyond . . . but fortified by digital.

Most importantly, these young and diverse leaders have led over 200 hacks on a range of increasingly strategic business challenges, and reverse mentored virtually every Nestlé executive. For example, they developed an "Uber of Kitchens" plan to leverage excess capacity of Nestlé kitchens for on-demand content, from videos to live streaming.

EXTERNAL "OUTSIDE-IN" INNOVATION

We also recognize that disruptive innovation is increasingly happening externally, and often from startups working at breakneck speed. With this in mind, we launched a *Silicon Valley Innovation Outpost,* or SVIO, in 2013, to help create a more effective and rapid "outside in" approach to innovation working with leading technology partners and especially promising early stage entrepreneurs. The team has a clear focus on Nestlé's strategic priorities. A primary goal is to identify and leverage leading partners to delight consumers and enhance their health and wellness.

We tackled this at the most basic level with a serious look at foundational service operations and support – 24/7 access, and responding quickly to all concerns, wherever the source. But our Innovation Outpost is pushing even harder on the "service" experience.

Let me illustrate. We were the first company to launch a program to help consumers learn more about what's behind the brand via QR code readers. But we struggled with adoption. One company we tested was Blippar, which allows us translate product and nutritional information to an augmented reality experience. We later fused this with a wearable strategy.

Let's also consider our popular Milo brand. With digital and content creating new rules of engagement, children are spending more and more time online rather than playing outside. Our MILO brand sought to innovate and retain its pioneering position on nutritious energy and teaching life values learned from sports. The MILO Champ band is the first fully integrated fitness tracker that syncs with a customized app. It helps parents track their child's activity and nutrition intake and encourages kids to be active and play more sports outdoors.

We are also piloting a solution that allows consumers to check on the health and wellbeing of their pets instantly through a urine test kit and their mobile phone. And we're collaborating with a number startups in the food delivery space in order to identify future e-commerce opportunities.

We're also better organizing for success. In July, we opened up our first office in San Francisco in a shared space with Swissnex. We intend to keep this lean – no more than 20 people. But lest you think our efforts are overly anchored to Silicon Valley, we do intend to work closely with other top innovation hubs, including, India, China, Berlin, London and other start-up hubs.

OPEN INNOVATION PLATFORM

We're also thinking well beyond geography. This year we launched Nestlé's first Open Innovation platform called HENRi@Nestlé. It's not a coincidence that the platform is named Henri. To bring a greater start-up spirit to our efforts, we have sought inspiration from a serial entrepreneur and innovator named Henri, the founder of Nestlé.

This Open Innovation platform will provide potential innovation partners with an attractive, compelling and seamless online platform that enables the rapid sharing of ideas, creative designs and innovative solutions in response to stated business challenges provided by internal stakeholders.

Through this platform we intend to change our mindset of "plan and perfect" to a dynamic "launch and learn." We want the platform to serve as the company's flagship, global collaboration program. And like the DAT, we expect it to serve as a catalyst for speed, transparency, and cutting red tape.

Honestly, I recall vividly – and painfully – how big customer bureaucracy nearly killed my startup. The product fit was perfect, but the speed was glacial. I'm obsessed with ensuring Nestlé doesn't frustrate or mismanage expectations with entrepreneurs. We need them. We *urgently* need them.

Through the development of Farine Lactee – the first infant formula, which was initially used to save a child – he effectively reached for a healthier future. Henri Nestlé's sense of scientific innovation, combined with an instinct for marketing and a global ambition continues to shape and drive the company today. The stakes are high. Indeed, our competition today is not merely the likes of Unilever & Mondelez but small start-ups transforming the food industry.

PULLING IT TOGETHER

Very little of what I've mentioned can work unless we're relentlessly connecting dots and sharing. Indeed, we see a huge upside in a more "connected and collaborative" Nestlé, ever committed to digital operating principles – especially sharing – to do more with less, and with greater impact.

There's no easy playbook here. My first effort to build an "internal community," back in 1999, was an abysmal failure. I spearheaded a high-minded initiative at P&G called "Marketing

Village." When it failed for lack of user adoption, my defensive instinct was to blame corporate naysayers, but the buck really stopped with me. I recklessly assumed technology alone would do the work. But, you can't just flip on a tech switch and expect things to happen. Building a community requires hands-on leadership, grounded to an ambition, plan, or even "naïve" ideal. I delegate many things, but not my Chatter groups, as I want my stamp on the community tenor, tone, and voice.

Transformation also sources from full immersion in the medium. I constantly repeat to my colleagues the phrase "Internal Master Drives External Mastery." To build great brands, we must be great communicators. Our communication must cut through noise and engage our targets across a fragmented media landscape. As we sell more products online, we must master real-time personalization, A/B testing, journey-mapping, shelf-positioning, and great *give and take* service.

Social media, internal or external, is a low-cost, feedback-rich testing environment. To transform the enterprise, leading by example is critical.

Remember, digital is at its core all about *better, faster, cheaper, smarter*. Leaders in this environment must be "end to end" in their thinking about its potential. In this way the manager can identify the critical gaps needed to accelerate, whether it's an internal startup team or an innovation outpost or an open-innovation platform.

FINAL COMMENTS

So yes, a large company can act like a start-up? For Nestlé, we're just getting warmed up on this realization. In fact, we named our Open Innovation platform HENRi to remind us that we're just getting warmed up on the next 150 years.

Let me close by reminding the reader that leadership – I repeat, *leadership* – is the most important building block of transformation. Great leadership treats every challenge as an opportunity, and can adapt to any environment. Good luck in your own journey.

CHAPTER 7

CONCLUSION

"Most large organizations embrace the idea of invention, but are not willing to suffer the string of failed experiments necessary to get there. Outsized returns often come from betting against conventional wisdom, and conventional wisdom is usually right. Given a ten percent chance of a 100 times payoff, you should take that bet every time. But you're still going to be wrong nine times out of ten. We all know that if you swing for the fences, you're going to strike out a lot, but you're also going to hit some home runs. The difference between baseball and business, however, is that baseball has a truncated outcome distribution. When you swing, no matter how well you connect with the ball, the most runs you can get is four. In business, every once in a while, when you step up to the plate, you can score 1,000 runs. This long-tailed distribution of returns is why it's important to be bold. Big winners pay for so many experiments." [1]

—Jeff Bezos, Founder, Amazon, 2015 Shareholder Annual Letter

THE ANSWER for surviving, and more importantly, thriving in this new digital economy does not come from a single strategy. The companies which remain on the Fortune 500 ten years from now will be the companies that leverage a mixture of tech acquisitions, investments in startups, innovative partnerships and even their own disruptive launches to transform their companies. While it will not be a single strategy that enables their survival, it also will not be a single effort.

Innovation is about repetition, while not dwelling on the experimentation that was unsuccessful. Thomas Edison, one the greatest innovators of all time, once said, "I have not failed 10,000 times – I've successfully found 10,000 ways that will not work." In fact, his guiding principle in life was: "Never get discouraged if you fail. Learn from it. Keep trying." This view on repetition and failure comes from the man that invented the light bulb, phonograph, and the motion picture. It also comes from the founder of Edison General Electric, a company we know today as

GE. The ultimate Blue Chip, GE was one of the original 12 companies listed on the newly formed Dow Jones Industrial Average in 1896. After 120 years, it is the only one of the original companies still listed on the Dow index. GE has been able to thrive for over a century because of the culture of experimentation that Edison set forth.

High stakes business is about the long-tailed distribution of returns that Bezos talks about. A company needs to experiment with innovation in order to have a chance to find the winners. For every breakaway success that Amazon has, like Prime, they have failed experiments like the Fire Phone, where the company was forced to write off $170 million on unsold phones. Some companies will wait so long to embrace the change that they will be forced into "bet the company" moves – the ones that give mergers and acquisitions a bad name. The smart companies will start to plant seeds knowing that some will grow and some will not. Those that do grow will turn into the big wins, paying for more than just the cost of the experiments.

> *If we don't create the thing that kills Facebook someone else will. Embracing change isn't enough. It has to be so hardwired into who we are that even talking about it seems redundant. The internet is not a friendly place. Things that don't stay relevant don't even get the luxury of leaving ruins. They disappear.*
> *—Facebook internal memo prior to IPO*

Companies and brands worldwide have a tremendous opportunity in front of them thanks to this innovation economy. There has probably never been a more exciting time to be in business as industries are created, destroyed, rebuilt, and reimagined in a matter of years. Digital is one of the greatest mediums ever created for marketers, but it is even more valuable for entrepreneurs and business leaders that see its transformative potential. Leveraging digital to its fullest requires change agents – those that will lead companies to embrace innovation and new approaches to management, product development, marketing, and business as a whole. The change cannot be isolated to a corporate innovation group. It cannot be outsourced to a Silicon Valley outpost or solved with immersion trips to visit digital innovators. The change needs to be led from within and embraced by leaders at each and every level of the organization. The time to act is now. I guarantee that somewhere in the world, there is an entrepreneur, startup, or even another big company, who is working on an innovative idea with the goal to reinvent your business. You can either be part of the change or let the change happen to you.

A NEW ERA BUILT ON ENTREPRENEURSHIP AND INNOVATION

With that in mind, I'll end with the words of Steve Blank from a post he wrote at the end of 2010. At that time, the world was still trying to recover from the financial crash of 2008. Unemployment in the U.S. had sky rocketed to over 10 percent. The Federal Reserve started a second round of "quantitative easing" hoping to stimulate the economy. In addition, a record 2.9 million U.S. properties received foreclosure filings that year. This time was also the backdrop when I decided to make the entrepreneurial leap, leaving P&G in September 2010 to join Rockfish and co-found The Brandery.

With the world facing an uncertain future, Blank wrote a post entitled "When It's Darkest, Men See the Stars" that spoke of the future:

"I believe that we will look back at this decade as the beginning of an economic revolution as important as the scientific revolution in the 16th century and the industrial revolution in the 18th century. We're standing at the beginning of the entrepreneurial revolution. This doesn't mean just more technology stuff, though we'll get that. This is a revolution that will permanently reshape business as we know it and more importantly, change the quality of life across the entire planet for all who come after us . . . It may be the dawn of a new era for a new American economy built on entrepreneurship and innovation."[2]

Writing this book a few years later, I think it is fair to say that Blank's vision for the future seems to be coming true. This new era built on entrepreneurship and innovation creates amazing opportunities in the world of high stakes business. It is up to all of us to embrace that and chart the path for the future of our industries in this new innovative world.

ACKNOWLEDGMENTS

This book has gone through many edits and rewrites to get to where it is today. A big thank you to Bryan Radtke and Jason Bender for reading the very rough first drafts. To Kenny Tomlin for being an inspiration on how the world of business is changing and helping me put that change into words. To Dawn Maire, Michael Stich, and Mike Orzali for all their inputs, builds, and thoughts. And finally to Craig Baldwin for pushing me to go for more than just "good enough" and inspiring the concept of high stakes.

When I started down the path of writing a book, I was fortunate to have many friends who took time out of their very busy schedules to share their advice from their own journeys in publishing. Thank you to Bob Gilbreath, Pete Blackshaw, Matt Britton, Michael Docherty, Jeffrey Rohrs, and Jim Stengel. Your advice was amazing and your writing inspired me to follow in your footsteps. Thank you as well to all the readers of Hard Knox Life over the years for making me believe that my writing was something people wanted to actually read.

The Rockfish team really brought this book to life. A big thanks to everyone who helped along the way, including Lauren Schultz, Rosie McGuire, Rick Neltner, Frank Melendez and Jamie Escudero.

The contributions and real-life stories from Gautam Gupta at Nature-Box, Brian Graves at Everything But The House, Rich Boehne at E.W. Scripps, and Pete Blackshaw at Nestle were the finishing touches. A big thank you to my fellow co-founders of The Brandery (JB Kropp, Bryan Radtke, and Rob McDonald) and all of the Brandery alumni who put their faith in us.

Most importantly, thank you to my family. You are the ones that motivate me in everything that I do. Thank you for putting up with every night that I was on the road instead of home with you. I could not have accomplished any of this without your support and love.

NOTES

CHAPTER 1

1. *Why Converse Decided To Mess With Success*; http://www.fastcompany.com/3048644/the-big-idea/chuck-it

2. https://www.google.com/patents/US4131919

3. http://lens.blogs.nytimes.com/2015/08/12/kodaks-first-digital-moment/

4. https://medium.com/newco/newco-shift-an-overview-5c020a919bb-f?mc_cid=b2f092fe01&mc_eid=94db51221e#.ffjbd6hj6

5. *Top 100 CPG Brands Mostly Lost Sales and Share in Past Year*; http://adage.com/article/cmo-strategy/top-100-cpg-brands-lost-sales-share-past-year/300660/

6. http://www.strategyand.pwc.com/global/home/what-we-think/innovation1000/top-innovators-spenders

7. http://techcrunch.com/2016/01/10/the-industrialists-dilemma/

8. http://www.hollywoodreporter.com/earshot/read-jimmy-iovines-usc-commencement-525328

9. *Disruption is better when it's other people's jobs*; https://m.signalvnoise.com/disruption-is-better-when-it-s-other-people-s-jobs-ad84098c3c6#.skukmi1sq

CHAPTER 2

1. http://www.globalcorporateventuring.com/article.php/12794/why-every-company-in-the-fortune-2000-will-have-a-venture-capital-arm

2. http://avc.com/2015/10/outsider-vs-disruptor/

3. https://twitter.com/levie/status/475787246885277696

CHAPTER 3

1. http://www.theatlantic.com/technology/archive/2016/01/the-decline-of-the-drivers-license/425169/

2. http://steveblank.com/2014/01/14/whats-a-pivot/

3. http://venturebeat.com/2016/03/04/at-100-bmw-sees-radical-new-future-in-world-of-driverless-cars/

4. http://fortune.com/2016/03/18/zipcar-founder-veniam/

5. https://www.cbinsights.com/blog/big-compay-ceos-execs-disruption-quotes/

6. http://www.dallasnews.com/business/retail/20160122-fossil-and-misfit-think-theyre-a-perfect-match.ece

CHAPTER 4

1. http://archive.fortune.com/magazines/fortune/fortune_archive/1999/11/22/269071/index.htm

2. http://archive.fortune.com/magazines/fortune/fortune_archive/1999/11/22/269071/index.htm

3. *Elon Musk and The Revenge of the Electric Car*; http://www.thedailybeast.com/articles/2011/04/25/elon-musk-of-tesla-motors-discusses-revenge-of-the-electric-car.html

CHAPTER 5

1. https://hbr.org/2002/03/making-sense-of-corporate-venture-capital

2. http://blog.8thandwalton.com/2013/07/walmart-supplier-glossary-jbp/

3. http://www.warc.com/LatestNews/News/EmailNews.news?ID=36392&
   Origin=WARCNewsEmail&CID=N36392&PUB=Warc_News&utm_
   source=WarcNews&utm_medium=email&utm_campaign=WarcNews
   20160315

4. http://www.warc.com/LatestNews/News/EmailNews.news?ID=36392&
   Origin=WARCNewsEmail&CID=N36392&PUB=Warc_News&utm_
   source=WarcNews&utm_medium=email&utm_campaign=WarcNews
   20160315

CHAPTER 7

1. http://phx.corporate-ir.net/phoenix.zhtml?TEXT=aHR0cDovL2FwaS
   50ZW5rd2l6YXJkLmNvbS9maWxpbmcueG1sP2lwYWdlPTEwODY
   wMjA1JkRTRVE9MCZTRVE9MCZTUURFU0M9U0VDVEElPTl9
   FTlRJUkUmc3Vic2lkPTU3&c=97664&p=irol-SECText#toc

2. https://steveblank.com/2010/11/24/when-its-darkest-men-see-the-stars/

INDEX

ABOUT THE AUTHOR

DAVE KNOX is Managing Director of WPP Ventures and Chief Marketing Officer of Rockfish, a WPP agency. Prior to Rockfish, Knox was a seven-year veteran of Procter & Gamble, where he was instrumental in the digital turnaround that led to P&G being named to *AdAge*'s Digital A-List. Dave was named to the iMedia 25 Class of Digital Innovators, CMO of the Year in the inaugural C-Suite Awards by Cincinnati Business Courier, and a "40 Under 40" by *AdAge* in 2015. Dave is a Managing Partner in the VC firm Vine St. Ventures and is the co-founder of The Brandery – one of the top ten startup accelerators in the country.